Catch the Burning Flag

Henry J. Hyde

November, 1974: The morning after HJH is first elected to Congress, the beginning of a 30-year journey. The flag is caught, but burns not.

Catch the Burning Flag:
Speeches and
Random Observations of
Henry Hyde

As life is action and passion, it is required of man that he should share the passion and action of his time, at peril of being judged not to have lived.

—Oliver Wendell Holmes, Jr.

To obtain more information, or to order bulk copies for educational or business uses, please contact:

National Review Books
215 Lexington Avenue
11th Floor
New York, NY 10016

www.nationalreview.com

ISBN: 0-9758998-1-3

Jacket and book design by Luba Myts

PRINTED IN THE UNITED STATES OF AMERICA

To my wife Judy,
who makes all things possible.

Acknowledgments

Woodrow Wilson is supposed to have said, "I not only use all the brains I have, but all that I can borrow." I have always tried to follow his example. As a result, it is impossible to identify every individual who has contributed to the ideas and convictions that animated my several decades in public service and gave form to the speeches that follow. The roster would include numerous congressional staffers, as well as many of my fellow Members, along with friends and informal counselors in the media, academic institutions, and Washington's proverbial think tanks. When I even try to list them, I am struck by the realization of how blessed I have been all these years to have been a part of such an illustrious and dedicated network of thinkers and activists.

With heartfelt appreciation for them all, I would like to pay special tribute where special gratitude is due. First, to my family, who lived through all my years of speechifying with patience and support. No words of mine are adequate to express either my debt to them or my affection for them. Speaking of affection, Robert Novak, who graciously condescended to write his own preface for this book, is sometimes called the Prince of Darkness. To those who know him well, he is simply a prince.

The smartest holders of high office are those who realize that a lot of people are smarter than they are. Accordingly, it was ever my wont, in preparing a major address, to seek the advice of people like George Fishman, Dan Freeman, Ann Kelly, Kathryn Lehman, Gardiner Peckham, Doug Seay, Sam Stratman, and others. The imprint of their counsel remains in many of the speeches that follow. In this regard, George Weigel's contributions over the years, with his gift for expression, cannot be adequately quantified.

Two people deserving of special acknowledgement are Tom Mooney and Tom Smeeton. Their incomparable contributions over the years include a warm friendship that I treasure. Also deserving of special mention is my Chief of Staff, Judy Wolverton, who was head of my district and Washington offices for thirty-two outstanding and productive years. Pat Durante and Alice Horstman provided the support in my district office that made lots of constituents happy. Their value to our office was beyond measure.

At National Review Books, Jack Fowler and his editorial team have been remarkably efficient and more than accommodating. My good friend, Bill Gribbin, whose facility gives this work much of its tone and scope, merits the compliment T. S. Eliot once gave to Ezra Pound: *Il miglior fabbro*, the better maker.

With all that said, whatever faults lie herein are mine. Even now, out of office, it is still my delight to share with readers the intellectual jostling of public policy debate. For ultimately it is the presentation of competing ideas—not money or ambition—that will shape our government, our society, and our future.

Henry Hyde
July, 2007

Election Night—the thrill of victory

Table of Contents

Center/forward for Georgetown, HJH would play a key defensive role in stopping George Mikan and defeating DePaul at Madison Square Garden in the 1943 NIT quarterfinals— considered one of the great upsets in college basketball history.

Introduction

Henry Hyde

There once was a time, a little more than a century ago, when there was a major market for collections of speeches. Way back then, people tended to care about words, and even more about oratory, which was a form of public entertainment. It was generally assumed that those in public life who used rhetoric actually meant something approximate to what they said. Schoolchildren were made to memorize, if not entire speeches, at least parts of this or that address—whether the splendidly lyrical one given at Gettysburg, or Bryan's magnificently wrong "Cross of Gold," or Webster's paean to the Union. Innumerable collections of speeches, from "statesmen" of an era when that appellation was used without irony, now molder away in old libraries across the land. Left to researchers of the obscure, and mice, their leather bindings dry-rot away, the gilding turns to dust, the pages crack and crumble.

How quaint it all seems now, in this era of instant celebrity for whichever White House speechwriter first claims credit, via a few press leaks, for a president's latest address. How quaint, indeed, at a time when the phrases of a planned speech are vetted beforehand through focus groups and media advisors. The young son of an old friend, having read Churchill's magisterial *History of the English Speaking Peoples*, asked why we don't have leaders who sound like Sir Winston. How to answer him? Because talking down is always easier than talking up? Or because mass entertainment has so debased our vocabulary, our sentence structure, and our attention span that we communicate better with slogans and gestures than with lofty language?

I exaggerate. Yet try to imagine Churchill revising a speech for fear that a line might be taken out of context in a hostile attack ad during the next election cycle. So we do not have anyone who sounds like Teddy Roosevelt or Thomas Hart Benton. Heck, we have no one who sounds like Ronald Reagan. We live, after all, in what might be called the Age of Deconstruction. I am referring not just to the prevailing academic ideology fomented by the theories of Jacques Derrida but, more broadly, to a prevailing cultural assumption: That the true meanings of what we say to one another cannot be found on our lips, but must be uncovered, as if we were peeling an onion, layer by layer, to get at the hidden reality. Hence the phenomenon of instant analysis, by which network interlocutors explain to the public the real meaning of what this or that public figure has just said. We no longer have to listen attentively; we can just wait for the eventual translation. There is, after all, general assent to the proposition that a politician is someone who can accuse his opponent of duplicity without appearing envious.

A second problem: Ours is also the Age of Irony. The preferred style for public, and indeed even for much personal, communication is a certain cool cleverness. If you've ever spoken passionately about something and had someone sarcastically respond, "Tell us what you really think," then you know what I mean. The implication is that you should be embarrassed to wear your heart on your sleeve. Emotional speech, severe speech, censorious speech is generally considered unsophisticated; and no one wants to be thought a hick. But there are times and subjects appropriate for political passion. There are offenses in the face of which one should not keep one's cool. Some deeds do need damning. So there may have been occasions—and they may be reflected in the pages that follow—when I have been unfashionably censorious. For which, in general, I remain unrepentant.

Which is not to suggest that we need not watch what we say, in speeches or otherwise. Early on in my congressional career, during one of our House debates on abortion, I referred to my opponents in a way that offended one of my colleagues, Congressman Les AuCoin, a Democrat from Oregon. He did me the favor, in an angry reaction to my words, to teach me an important lesson. I had intended to convince, but instead I had alienated. I recall apologizing to him at the time, and I would like now to extend the same mea culpa to anyone else to whom my rhetoric may have been biting rather than persuasive.

Against all those considerations, it may be folly to present herewith . . . a collection of speeches. This does not seem to reflect smart market analysis. Today's readers might well prefer the latest forward-looking campaign bio to a rerun of yesteryear's arguments—until they realize that this year's crop of presidential hopefuls are trying to deal with the same problems, by and large, that some of us have tackled for the last several decades. For my part, I am not running for anything these days. Much of the time, I just lounge in a rather comfortable chair. Tennessee Williams' sweet bird of youth just whispers her notes to me now. So I need not try to make this book an I-can-solve-it-all compendium of every issue that might be raised with a White House aspirant on a weekend interview show. For an exercise of that magnitude, I have neither the staff nor the ambition nor the audacity. I can only say about those contenders, of both parties, who are continually discovering new solutions to more and more problems, more power to them. Which, by the way, is precisely what they are after. (Pardon an aside. This country needs a word, a category, to apply to persons who are credible presidential hopefuls. In the Catholic Church, one refers to potential popes as "papabile." I have been unable to come up with a counterpart term for our political pontificators. Ovalofficiables? Commanderables? The question does bear study.)

It is commonly said that the world completely changed on September 11, 2001. It did not. As devastating as that day was to all of us, as much as our own lives have been affected since then, the world, in the larger course of history, has altered not much at all. Evil men still do evil things, innocent millions suffer, good people make a difference where and when they can. Noting those facts is neither determinism nor despair. It is maturity. And since the roots of our present troubles bore deep into the past, it may be useful to revisit the debates of that past, perhaps to find therein some insight that could make the present a bit clearer.

Using the past in any form has become risky business in American politics. Historical allusions fall on deaf ears, the result of public education's virtual abandonment of the teaching of history. We've all heard the horror stories—and they are horrors!—about school textbooks which focus on radicals, dissenters, and kooks to the neglect of major national figures. Then along comes someone like David McCulloch with his biography of John Adams, restoring our second president to the stature he merited, and the reading public responds with enthusiasm. A few score historians like McCulloch, and we might in time reeducate the American people about their own heritage. In the meantime, it is risky for a speech-giver to presume a common body of historical knowledge among one's audience. One example should suffice. A few years back, the speechwriter for a nationally-known congressional leader of my own party put into his boss's text a reference to Norman Thomas, the most prominent American socialist of the Twentieth Century. As a perennial candidate for the presidency, an icon of the international Left, Thomas lived long enough to see much of his program enacted into law, piecemeal, in the name of liberal reform. Always defeated at the polls, he won big time at the tally of history. Even so, the staffer had to delete Norman Thomas from the speech when he discovered that the boss had never heard of him. Oops.

The same, even more woefully, holds true with regard to this country's constitutional development. When was the last time you heard a Member of Congress base his or her opposition to a bill purely on constitutional grounds? There's a reason for that dearth of argument. These elected folks know what sells; they know what the voters back home will take seriously. And since there is virtually no public education about the content of the Constitution—its Bicentennial in 1988 was one of the great lost opportunities for relearning—appealing to the separation of powers, or the limitation of the courts, or First Amendment rights against various campaign "reforms," comes across as disingenuous, a mere excuse for opposition. Were a Member of Congress today to give an impassioned speech on the House floor about an unconstitutional provision of a pending bill, it might be thought a little odd.

What, after all, is there to get excited about when we've all been taught that the Constitution is a living document, the fine print of which is rarely read by the citizens who live under its protections.

It is admirable that many Members of Congress carry with them a pocket-sized copy of the Constitution, as a reminder of their solemn responsibilities under that document. Sad to say, the text they carry is hardly a reliable expression of current constitutional policy. For that, we must turn to the case law, those frequent court-inspired interpretations of what the framers *really* meant, no matter what they actually said. For more than half a century, the most important source of social policy in America has been neither the people nor their elected officials, but the Supreme Court. The Justices have imposed their own image on our country, largely by reinterpreting four words in the Fourteenth Amendment: "due process" and "equal protection." The result—government by unelected judges—constitutes a legal assault on our Constitution, something which demands much more attention than it receives from most of my fellow citizens.

But let me get back to those old volumes of antiquated speeches, the collected wisdom of congressional solons, religious leaders, cultural figures, most of whose names now ring no bells. It is naive for their counterparts today to think their fame will last longer, no matter how finely spun are our speeches or how energetic may be our publishers. In America's disposable society, we all have a short shelf-life. I am reminded of a member of President Reagan's original White House staff who, while his colleagues were decorating their West Wing offices with paintings borrowed from the National Gallery of Art, posted on his wall only these lines from Elliot's "Prufrock":

> *No! I am not Prince Hamlet, nor was meant to be;*
> *Am an attendant lord, one that will do*
> *To swell a progress, start a scene or two,*
> *Advise the prince; no doubt, an easy tool,*
> *Deferential, glad to be of use,*
> *Politic, cautious, and meticulous;*
> *Full of high sentence but a bit obtuse;*
> *At times, indeed, almost ridiculous—*
> *Almost, at times, the Fool.*

Smart fellow, to have realized it at the start of the game, rather than at the finish line, as so many belatedly do. After 32 years in the Congress, after chairing both the Judiciary Committee and the Foreign Affairs Committees of the House, after managing the impeachment of one president and the defense against impeachment of another (in the Iran-Contra affair), I know I am no Prince of Denmark.

On the other hand, if, for our little whiles, through whatever historical happenstance, we do gain the public's attention, we should make the most of that fickle spotlight. And if, for a little while, it is thought that we have something worthwhile to say, then by all means we have an obligation to say it. In doing so, we may provoke some discussion, perhaps even some correction from which we ourselves can realize our earlier misjudgments. Certainly my opponents on many of the great issues of the last several decades—and they were opponents, not enemies—will find herein ample reason to justify their dissent from opinions of my thinking.

Some may consider the speeches in this book ideological. I like to think of them as thoughtful. For let it be said, and emphasized, that ideology and reason are complements, not opposites. They clash only when one or the other is defective. There is such a thing as being so reasonable that you cannot take action against even the gravest ills, or being so ideological that you cannot see the ills you are imposing upon others. Which is to say, I don't want to preach to the choir; I do not want to preach at all. I do ask for a hearing, because even my advanced middle age, as I begin my ninth decade, has not altered my commitment to the causes and principles that shaped the speeches which follow. The men and women with whom it was my honor to stand, to fight, occasionally to win, they need not fear any lessening of my beliefs or any diminution of my optimism that those beliefs will in the end prevail. I offer them this assurance I've borrowed from Robert Frost: "They would not find me changed from him they knew—Only more sure of all I thought was true."

Foreword

Robert Novak

T   he only mention of me in this collection by my old friend Henry Hyde is his noting the one issue on which we ever had serious disagreements: term limits. He correctly lists me as "one of the most zealous advocates" for limiting how long members of Congress can serve, while he was a passionate foe of such restrictions.

In truth, however, I never would have been at odds with Henry on this issue if other elected politicians were more like him. I concede that Henry Hyde is the greatest living argument against term limits. It would have been the nation's loss had he been prevented from serving his full thirty-two years in the House of Representatives. The problem for me is that he has been an island of skill and integrity in a sea of mediocrity and corruption.

These speeches reflect a rare combination of eloquence and erudition, and something more. In an age of increasing specialization on Capitol Hill, Henry Hyde was the Renaissance man there. Readers of this book must be impressed by the breadth and variety of his expertise. Considering the liberal assault on Hyde as a Catholic extremist who keeps poor women from abortions and persecuted Bill Clinton, the tone here may come as a surprise to some. These selections are free of Republican partisanship and remarkably non-ideological.

A collected book of speeches is rare in 21st Century American politics because hardly any members of today's political class have anything to say that is worth putting between hard covers. It is painful even to contemplate reading the pabulum passing for oratory—tired rhetoric distilled from partisan talking points. I cannot think of more than two or three sitting members of Congress who conceivably would publish a collection of their speeches that anyone other than members of their immediate families would want to read.

Hyde delivered two of the rare speeches in the contemporary

House that were recalled beyond the moment of their presentation: one in behalf of a constitutional amendment against flag burning, and the other against term limits. In each, he was able to take two unpopular causes derided by the liberal establishment (the news media in particular) and elevate them with the combination of eloquence and scholarship that that has marked his Congressional oratory.

By the time his "Catch the Burning Flag" speech was delivered in 1990, Hyde had become a distinguished House member in his fifteenth year in Congress who by his intellect and personality had won admiration on both sides of the aisle. He easily could have avoided what he called (in his famous June 21, 1990, speech to the House) "the slings and arrows of the media, which relentlessly condemns us as cultural lags and political pygmies for our alleged weakness in caving in to the populist patriotic notions of the American people."

But Hyde felt there was a philosophical point to be made. Henry was surely the only participant in the House debate to reach back to the excesses of the French Revolution to justify protecting the flag:

> Remember, when everything is permitted, and nothing is forbidden, we are heeding the ghost of Robespierre, not Jefferson or Madison. We do not understand freedom if we do not understand responsibility. For every right, there is a correlative duty. But though we have a Bill of Rights, we lack a Bill of Duties. We have ten amendments that guarantee us all kind of rights. How about one amendment that says we have a duty, not to respect the flag or to love it, but just not to destroy or defile it? Is that too much to ask, one duty? The law, it is said, is a teacher, and it should be a teacher here.

Delivering the anti-term limits speech was even more antithetical to the politics of expediency practiced in the House of Representatives. Term limits was featured prominently among the many promises contained in Newt Gingrich's "Contract with America," the House Republican platform for the successful 1994 campaign. In fact, neither the Speaker nor any of the other

Republican leaders had the slightest intention of passing term limits. Under their cleverly orchestrated procedure, every Republican would get a chance to vote for some variety of term limits and even deliver a favorable speech if so desired, but absolutely nothing would pass. Obviously, senior Republican members definitely were not supposed to be speaking in opposition.

Henry, unwilling to have any part of this charade, delivered his speech on February 12, 1997. It still is recalled by those who heard it as a declaration of faith in politics as a serious profession:

> This is no place for amateurs. A Congressman who makes a career of public service, and who is willing to make the sacrifices that entails, develops a record. That record is a standard of comparison to be judged by. From election to election, he is accountable for the long-term consequences of his actions. No hobbyist legislator, no part-time lame duck legislator can share that motivation.

Certainly, the printed page cannot truly reflect the oratory of Henry Hyde, particularly when speaking from the well of the House: a towering, hulking, white-maned presence with his slightly high-pitched but resonant voice filling the chamber. "He's a rare member," Vice President Dick Cheney, his former colleague in the House, said at Hyde's retirement dinner in September 2006, "who can bring the House to silence merely by stepping to the well."

Nor can the printed page capture Henry Hyde's comic talents. He is genuinely witty, a rare quality for a practicing politician in any era but especially today. As executive producer of CNN's "Capital Gang," I picked him as the outside guest on our annual light-hearted Christmas program when the panelists had to think up satirical guests for prominent public figures. He never failed.

Contact with Hyde in Congress was always a delight and often a surprise, as when he would suddenly break into song to serenade his long-suffering press aide Sam Stratman with a rendition of "Sam, You Made the Pants Too Long!"

Traces of that style appear in this volume, as in his impatience with the "youthful exuberance" of Republican colleagues carrying the banner of reform after they gained control of the House in the

1994 elections. He writes here that "there is every reason to be skeptical of most reformist projects, especially those which would alter the structure of the Congress or the Constitution, when they are undertaken with the same jejune frivolity with which the teenaged Judy Garland and Mickey Rooney would cry, 'Let's put on a show.'"

I can't imagine many of Henry's sober-sided Republican compatriots appreciating that analogy, much less any of them conceiving it. But he stood out from them in many other ways. Prior to the 1970s, Republicans with Henry Hyde's background were not seen in Congress. He is the quintessential Reagan Democrat.

Henry was raised by working class parents in Chicago as a Roman Catholic and a Democrat. The fact that he stood 6-foot-3 and was an excellent basketball player was his ticket out of obscurity and into a career that he could hardly imagine. His record at St. George's high school earned him a basketball scholarship at Georgetown University in Washington, D.C., a Catholic college seeking a place in the basketball sun and signing a recruit from Chicago for the first time.

The 18-year-old boy was fascinated by the nation's capital, and he soon found what it was like to be in the national spotlight. The Georgetown team was considered a hopeless underdog in the 1943 national collegiate semifinals at New York's Madison Square Garden against a great DePaul team from Chicago led by the all-time All-American 6-foot-10 center George Mikan. Hyde was a reserve guard playing his first year of varsity basketball as a sophomore. But he convinced his coach that he had the number of his towering fellow Chicagoan Mikan and could contain him. In fact, he held Mikan down for the last ten minutes, and Georgetown scored a stunning upset. For the first time, "Hank" Hyde found his name in newspapers across the country. As an omen for the future, he had fought an uphill battle against the odds—and fought it effectively.

For the next basketball season, Hyde was a junior naval officer commanding a LCT (landing craft) in the South Pacific, dodging deadly Japanese kamikaze suicide planes. That, too, was to set him aside from most Congressional colleagues, as a combat veteran with a deeper realization of what war meant.

After earning a post-war law degree from Loyola University in Chicago, Hyde voted for Dwight D. Eisenhower for president in 1952 and officially became a Republican in 1958. The Democrats no longer fit what Hyde viewed as the proper U.S. posture confronting the Soviet threat. He ran for Congress from a Northwest Chicago district in 1962 and lost, but was elected to the Illinois General Assembly in 1966. A natural leader, he became House Majority Leader during eight years in Springfield, and tried again for Congress in 1974 a dozen years after his failure. This time he ran in a suburban district, and he was elected.

Hyde was 50 when he arrived on Capitol Hill, a little old for a freshman trying to make his mark in the House. It took another eight years for him to get a seat on the Foreign Affairs Committee, to pursue his overriding interest in protecting the nation's security in the Cold War. Henry was 58 years old in 1983, at the end of the committee table with Republicans sill entombed in the minority after another election in which the Democrats gained seats in the House.

But Henry Hyde never fit the mold of the back-bench Republican, content to have been elected to Congress with all its attendant perquisites. Defying the old rule that freshmen legislators should not be seen if it all possible and certainly never be heard, he inscribed his name forever in the history books in 1976, his second year in Congress. He somehow won passage of the Hyde Amendment, prohibiting federal Medicaid funds to finance abortion. Each Congress since then has seen the Hyde Amendment passed again and again.

Thus did an unknown lawyer from Illinois instantly became a national—indeed, an international—icon of the pro-life movement. His speech to the House on September 19, 1996, pleading for an override of President Bill Clinton's veto of the partial birth abortion bill, reflected his passion.

> This debate has been about an unspeakable horror. And while the details are graphic and grisly, it has been, I think, helpful for all of us, and for our country, to recognize the full brutality of what goes on in America's aborturaries, day in and day out, week

after week, month after month, year after year. We are not talking about abstractions here. We are talking about life and death at their most elemental.

The startling reality is that Hyde was not elected to the Republican leadership for eighteen years, which is testimony to the character of his colleagues rather than his. In 1993, he finally became chairman of the Republican Policy Committee, fourth-ranking in the party hierarchy. When Republicans gained control of the House in the 1994 elections, Speaker-designate Gingrich asked Hyde to take the chairmanship of the important Judiciary Committee—jumping over one more senior member who clearly was unqualified for the post. That meant Hyde had to give up his leadership, which may have been the real purpose for the shift.

Whatever the purpose of moving Hyde, its eventual unintended consequence was to propel him into the impeachment of William Jefferson Clinton. At first, Hyde said impeachment should not be pursued unless it were bipartisan. But he came to consider crimes committed by the President to be so serious that he must proceed, even without Democratic assistance.

The result was Henry Hyde at his best, as an orator and advocate while serving as principal House manager of the impeachment proceedings. His performance climaxed February 8, 1999, with his magnificent closing argument to the Senate. It should be required reading for Americans who believe the case against Clinton was based only on sexual misconduct. To Senators ready to acquit the President, Hyde said:

> You're saying a perjurer and an obstructor of justice can be president in the face of no less than three precedents for conviction of federal judges for perjury. You shred these precedents and you raise the most serious questions of whether the President is in fact subject to the law, or whether we are beginning a restoration of the divine rights of kings.

After six mostly turbulent years heading the Judiciary Committee, Hyde faced the Gingrich-imposed rule limiting

Republican committee chairmen to three two-year terms. Hyde's requested waiver to stay at Judiciary was denied. Ironically, that disappointment enabled him to become chairman of the House Committee on International Relations (the Foreign Affairs Committee before and after the twelve years of Republican control). So Hyde concentrated on his first priority—the national security of the United States—during his last six years in Congress. He had told me in 1987 when there was a vacancy at the CIA, he was willing to leave his seat in Congress to become Director of Central Intelligence if asked. He was not asked. The mess at the CIA might have been cleaned up if he were.

Hyde's new chairmanship and George W. Bush's new presidency were both only two months old when on March 7, 2001, he presided over the first appearance before the International Relations Committee by Secretary of State Colin Powell. The Cold War had been won, the Nine/Eleven terrorist attacks were in the future and Republicans had just won control of both the executive and legislative branches for the first time in fifty-two years. But in his opening remarks published here, Chairman Hyde is not triumphant. Rather, he is concerned about what lies ahead for the United States as the sole surviving superpower.

> Despite our power, we must resist the temptation of believing we can fix every problem, indulge in every wish. Part of our strategy must be to decide what we cannot do, what we choose not to do and to ensure that others take up responsibilities...
>
> [A] practical, long-term vision is sorely needed. It is a prerequisite that we dare not postpone until some more convenient time. I say this not as a Republican. Indeed, there is no hope of success unless it is broadly bipartisan. We need consensus in this body and in this city, as well as the support of the American people.

Hyde had a presentiment of what was ahead, but President Bush paid him no heed. That warning reflected the real Henry Hyde—prudent, free of partisan cant, and insightful.

I miss his presence in Congress for personal reasons of friendship, but also because of the void left by his absence. Who will be steadfast in defense of the unborn? Who will take up the cause of Christians in the Holy Land? Who will care about the fight against Colombia's narco-terrorists?

Henry Hyde is irreplaceable, perhaps indispensable. But I still disagree with him on term limits.

Robert D. Novak
Washington, D.C.

Congress
and
Reform

HJH sworn in as a new Congressman in 1975 (located appropriately just right of center, to the right of son Tony)

The three speeches in this chapter concern the Congress, to which I came in January 1975 in the wake of Watergate and where I experienced, as so many new Members do, congressional culture shock. I had been in Washington before, in 1942, as a teenager from Chicago with a basketball scholarship to Georgetown University, where I would spend a year before enlisting in the Navy. In 1946, with the war over and a discharge as a lieutenant junior grade, I returned to Georgetown to complete my studies. So I knew well the special romance of Washington and how its history always moved me. Now I was going to be one of those players upon the grand stage, though I could not possibly have envisioned the events that lay ahead for me and for our country.

Four days later, I joined my new colleagues in the House chamber to hear President Ford deliver his State of the Union address, unaware of how ill prepared I was for some of the realities of my new job. Eight years in the Illinois legislature had not taught me about the intense partisanship, the towering egos, or the sheer numbers of Congress. It struck me that this legislative body was an unwieldy beast that moved in its own direction in its own good time.

That January was not a propitious time for anyone to begin an education as a freshman Member of the House. That kind of learning should take place in a positive atmosphere, but the national mood had seldom been more negative. Just five months earlier, President Nixon had resigned after the House Judiciary Committee voted in favor of impeachment proceedings. Communist forces were continuing their attacks against the Saigon government in violation of the 1973 Paris Agreement. Abandoned by the United

States, the South Vietnamese rightly feared a total defeat. America's helicopter retreat from the roof of our Embassy, from Vietnam, and from honor was only three months away.

We had no way of knowing that the Communist conquest of Vietnam would be a deathbed triumph—one of its last. Nor did anyone foresee that just six years ahead, the election of Ronald Reagan would restore our national self-respect and begin the process that would culminate in the dissolution of the USSR. To paraphrase the ancient declamation: O Lenin, where is thy sting; Stalin, where is thy victory? By the same token, we cannot now know whether our country's currently dire situation will turn for the better or worse. Either way, there are today 54 House freshmen, elected for the first time in November 2006, who will have to make their way through it all, one day at a time, just as I did when I was in their shoes.

As I was mulling over this introduction, those newly elected men and women of the 110th Congress were coming to Washington for their first briefings before taking office. (And many of them were discovering that their families would not be able to live in the Washington area because of its extraordinary housing costs, but that's another matter.) They were coming to the same institution to which I had come as a freshman more than three decades earlier: the People's Chamber, as we like to style it. Its physical surroundings have changed very little since 1975. Its physical production— the bills, resolutions, its legislative calendar, the stationery, and so on—are timeless in their appearance. The marble, the statues, the paintings, that great dome that still inspires awe for the majesty of our democracy—all this bespeaks a permanence beyond the winds of political change. But inside that Capital, some important things have changed considerably.

Most obvious has been the demographic change. I don't mean simply the arrival of several dozen women and a far larger contingent of minority members than in earlier days; everyone is aware of that transformation. Less immediately evident is an age differential. There are far fewer older members of the House nowadays. Although some of its most effective members are old hands like John Dingell of Michigan and Tom Lantos of California, congressional service is increasingly a young persons game, for several reasons. First, there is just so much more work to be done. Occasional junkets—rather, fact-finding trips—aside, for most members their daily responsibilities outrun the time available to do them. There are simply too many committee meetings, mark-ups, speeches, floor votes, constituent conferences, drop-bys, media appearances, home district events—and occasional visits with the spouse and kids. Even if one is blessed with a politically "safe" district—in which, for whatever reasons, the incumbent has virtually a lifetime hold on the seat—congressional service is physically challenging, more so now, I believe, than when I arrived during the presidency of Gerald Ford.

One reason, of course, is that the Congress, like the rest of the federal government, has expanded its scope far beyond its intended limits. Like a five-year-old left unattended, we do tend to get into everything. The more issues, the more opportunities to act. The more crises, the more dramatic responses. The more all this builds up, the less competently can it be handled. For example, there will never be enough time in Congress's schedule to exercise properly its oversight authority over the hundreds of bureaucratic programs it has created within the executive branch. Why do so many of them run out of control? For the same reason a dog without a leash wanders onto your lawn.

Consider the perennial proposals to "reform" the IRS code (setting aside the fact that one man's reform is another's oppression). Almost every recent Congress has enacted some significant change to the federal tax system. But it has been decades since the Congress took up a comprehensive tax bill in a way that Members would have the opportunity—or the necessity—to vote on any and all parts of the code through unlimited amendments thereto. There are few Members, in House or Senate, who have ever had that experience. Who in today's Senate, for example, could replicate the Herculean work of Russell Long and Carl Curtis, as Chairman and Ranking Minority Member of the Senate Finance Committee, when they managed the Tax Reform Bill of 1976, with its scores of amendments taking weeks of debate on the Senate floor? How many Senators, moreover, would be eager to cast that many votes on specific tax proposals, thereby alienating this or that interest group? No, things have to made simpler, more streamlined, to fit the schedule of course, and to spare Members the ordeal of mastering—much less defending—several hundred provisions of the IRS code. So it is that today's Congress changes our tax laws under cover of the Budget Process (a "reform" adopted just before I began my congressional career). Within that budget regimen, Congress does battle over taxes through competing budget resolutions; it's almost a proxy fight. Its outcome, however, makes it possible for the winning side to later enact its preferred tax legislation under strict time limitations and severe limits on debate and amendments. When it comes to your federal taxes, you see, there can be such a thing as too much democracy; but the rules of the Budget Process solve that problem.

The use of the Budget Process as a winner-take-all substitute for customary legislative procedure was brought to perfection by President Reagan's Director of the Office of Management and Budget, former Congressman David Stockman. Whatever his failings, he was certainly one of the cleverest people in the Reagan White House and, in the first days of that Administration, came up with its successful strategy of packaging the President's economic program, supply-side tax cuts and all, as one humongous Budget vote. And that's been the pattern ever since. Win the vote on the Budget, and you hold the high cards—especially in the form of time limits in the Senate—for the rest of the year. Until, that is, the appropriation bills come along, with emergency appropriations and supplemental appropriations too, and raise the question of whether the Budget Process has really done any good for the Congress and the nation.

So it usually is with structural changes that fail to address underlying problems. They complicate instead of curing. The classic examples of this come from the Progressive Era of the early Twentieth Century, when true believers in some states established the processes we know as initiative and referendum to enact or repeal laws, voter recall of Members of Congress, and the direct election of senators mandated by the Seventeenth Amendment to the Constitution. All those changes had considerable merit, with the reservation that recall of congressmen is almost surely unconstitutional; yet its mere mention by some conservatives during the Panama Canal debate of 1977 created angry panic in some quarters. But in today's highly ideological politics, initiatives and referenda—many of which I heartily support—clutter state ballots like litter in an urban alley. And who is to say whether the direct election of senators, having taken that choice out of the presumably untrustworthy hands of state legislatures, has not resulted in a media-driven, image-conscious, less substantive and more pandering form of politics. The voters wanted more control over the Senate; what they got was more charisma.

Even so, there is a persistent magic in the word reform, no matter how many crimes are committed in its name. No wonder that Emerson, ordinarily the soul of optimism, observed that "every reform is only a mask under cover of which a more terrible reform, which dares not yet name itself, advances." (Memo to certain Justices of the Supreme Court: Read Emerson.) I am not that jaundiced about the possibility of progress; and indeed I recognize the wisdom in the adage, "We must reform if we would conserve," even though that comes from Franklin Roosevelt, about whom my enthusiasm has always been limited.

Still, there is every reason to be skeptical of most reformist projects, especially those which would alter the structure of the Congress or the Constitution, when they are undertaken with the same jejune frivolity with which the teenaged Judy Garland and Mickey Rooney would cry, "Let's put on a show!" That youthful exuberance erupted during those heady months of planning, and then implementing, the Republican Revolution of 1994, when there was talk of doubling the size of the House of Representatives (to put Members in closer touch with their public) and of having Members vote on legislation from their district offices (presumably so that the local media could literally look over our shoulders to make sure we weren't on the take.)

What can one say? These whacko plans contravened the very nature of our assembly. We were, after all, supposed to be a congrex—literally a flock coming together—not a mere tally board of conflicting yeas and nays. To do serious legislative work, we needed to be able to look one another in the eye, grab onto a shoulder, exchange a handshake that is more binding than a written contract, and confidentially tell a colleague he doesn't know what he's talking about. We needed the private conversations, the wheeling and dealing that could actually get things done by such publicly difficult tactics as compromise, learning, and admitting we were wrong. And even in an assembly of 435 disparate individuals, we needed a certain level of intimacy, of familiarity with one another, if we were to conduct the nation's business well. In the end, everyone forgot about doubling the House size and voting from back home. I fear, nonetheless, that our Congress is becoming an intermittent gathering of strangers, too busy to maintain the personal ties that sustain an institution in times of conflict and crisis.

Reforming government is now a continuing enterprise, though its successes seem always to defy quantification. Constant reform, like constant dieting, is its own admission of defeat. It is rather like the old saw, perpetual war for perpetual peace. There is no way to demonstrate that it is not working, because, by its very failure, it uncovers new problems in need of its continuance. Under Republican auspices in 1995, the House created a permanent subcommittee on Government Reform. Its perpetual mandate was meant to emphasize our commitment to forcing positive change upon the Executive Branch, but that same mandate can also be interpreted as a confession that the scores of other House subcommittees can't really be expected to do that job within their respective jurisdictions. I think it was Roscoe Conklin, the Nineteenth Century Senator from New York, who observed that, when Samuel Johnson made his famous remark about patriotism being the last refuge of a scoundrel, he failed to consider the possibilities of the word "reform."

This is just one example of a phenomenon omnipresent in contemporary politics: When something isn't working well, we don't replace it; we add to it. This is one reason why there are so many overlapping and duplicative programs within the Executive Branch. It is also why, at certain levels, incompetence is less likely to be purged than to be circumvented. As long as payroll is no problem, it's easier to hire than to fire. And so does government grow—and not just government. Anyone who has worked in major corporations or large professional firms has probably witnessed this same syndrome. It is, I think, characteristic of fat, aging institutions; and it makes those institutions prime targets for hostile takeovers and downsizing.

Not that anyone is about to downsize the Congress, although there was brave talk on that point during the so-called Republican Revolution of 1994, when some reductions were actually accomplished. In fact, early in 1993, the Republican *minority*, through sheer audacity and persistence, had forced the abolition of four select committees of the House. Someday someone must write the full account of how that totally unexpected triumph transformed a whipped minority, suddenly bereft of Executive Branch assistance with the fall of the Bush-Quayle Administration, into an energized and determined cadre hell-bent on winning control of the House. And when they do, they will discover an idealistic staff member who, shall we say, kicked down the first domino. Lincoln is supposed to have called Harriet Beecher Stowe "the little lady who started the big war." I propose the same compliment for Dr. Carol Statuto Bevin, a distinguished authority in issues pertaining to youngsters, whose determination to end the anti-family charades of the Democrat-controlled House Select Committee on Children, Youth, and Families became the catalyst for so much that followed thereafter.

Healthy institutions—whether innovative companies, flexible military units, cutting-edge research networks, successful teaching teams—always have individuals like her. A hallmark of such institutions is that, if a component is not functioning as it should, out it goes; for there is too much risk and too few resources to lard on another layer. That is true reform. Someday it may be applied to our national government. But the key is always the same: getting the

right people, not changing the system; empowering the right individuals, not altering time-tested structures.

All of which puts the responsibility for reform right back where
it belongs: with the voters who do the most important hiring and fir-
ing in the Congress. President Garfield is best remembered, when
he is remembered at all, as the victim of an assassin. He deserves
better, if only for having had the guts to say this: "Now, more than
ever before, the people are responsible for the character of their
Congress. If that body be ignorant, reckless, and corrupt, it is
because the people tolerate ignorance, recklessness and corruption.
If it be intelligent, brave, and pure, it is because the people demand
these high qualities to represent them in the national legislature."

I will take that as my cue to discuss briefly the three speeches
that compose this chapter, for they all deal with that relationship
between Members of Congress and the people they represent.
Elected officials should always be receptive to new ways to do their
jobs, especially as changes both demographic and technological
rush us into new territory, so to speak, in the expansion of our
democratic culture. Perhaps it has always been so. In the majestic
Archives building on Pennsylvania Avenue, tourists line up and
wait their turn to glimpse, encased in a nuclear-bomb proof vault,
the originals of the Declaration of Independence and the
Constitution. While those priceless pages are venerated in their
great hall, elsewhere in the building's dim and dusty recesses lie
yellowed pages that testify, in their own homespun way, to the
vitality of freedom in the early American Republic. These are
"instructions," not petitions, sent to one or another Member of
Congress by meetings of constituents, telling him how he should
vote on a matter of critical importance.

The idea that the folks back home should be able to dictate a
Member's vote was an early expression of plebiscitary, rather than
representative, democracy. After decades spent reading my own
constituent mail, I can testify that the desire for direct popular management of a Member's decisions still runs strong. And yet, it is
contrary to the philosophical basis of our system of government.
The role of an elected representative—note that I did not say "mes-

senger"—is the subject of the first speech that follows this introduction: my remarks to newly elected Members of Congress in
November, 1990. I recall it came as something like shock therapy
to some in the audience, and its emphasis upon the independence of
Members may not go down easy with some readers.

The speech thereafter is sure to lose me some friends. I regret
that, though I do not regret the speech. My opposition to constitutionally imposed term limits disappointed many, and only with a
heavy heart did I break ranks with so many allies and counselors. I
would, however, do it again.

The third address herein is my brief farewell, in September
2006, to the institution that was my life and love for 32 years—hard
years, most of them, with bruises that will never stop aching and
losses beyond retrieval. But they were wonderful years, peopled by
so many heroic men and women, so many noble individuals, so
many champions of right and justice and compassion. So many
Americans, for whom I will ever give thanks.

November 29, 1990

Remarks to Newly Elected Members of Congress

Welcome to the city of the superlative; everything here is either outstanding or outrageous. You can leave nuance back home.

As newly elected Members of the House of Representatives, you are in the throes of a thoroughly exhilarating experience, ranking right up there with Churchill's being shot at and missed.

Someone once said that the greatest experience in the world is to do good by stealth—and then to be discovered by accident. (Perhaps that is what press secretaries are for.) But just getting elected to Congress is quite an accomplishment, and you are each entitled to enjoy a few moments devoid of the cynicism that pervades this town.

One of my favorite cynics was the late Senator Eugene McCarthy, who once said that a politician has to be like a football coach, smart enough to know something about the game but dumb enough to think that what he's doing is important. Each of you is plenty smart already, or else you wouldn't be here. As for whether what you do here is going to be important, well, that will be entirely up to you.

I have ransacked my files for the precise quotation, the best press clipping, the sharpest idea I could share with you that would help you the most in coping with the stresses your new career will impose. (Remember, when you use one person's words, it's plagiarism; but when you quote many people, it's called research.) So I researched from Pericles to Vince Lombardi, from Dostoevsky to Casey Stengel, and I could not find any wisdom that I could impart with credibility and authenticity. So instead, I want to convey to you, at this sumptuous luncheon, my own secret of immense value and utility. It's simply this: You do not have to swallow everything they put in front of you!

And I am not speaking of the food.

My first word to you really should have been congratulations. Congratulations for taking the risk of running for public office. Congratulations for enduring a campaign with all its difficulties and vulnerabilities. Congratulations on your election to the people's Chamber, the House of Representatives. Fashionable cynicism notwithstanding, public service like yours is a vocation capable and deserving of honor. Because the law is a teacher as well as a boundary-setter, it is no overstatement to say that your work in Congress will help shape the course of the great and ongoing experiment in American self-government.

By your actions and your decisions, you will help answer the question that Lincoln posed to his, and to succeeding, generations of Americans, the question of whether a nation "so conceived and so dedicated can long endure." The way we answer that question will shape not only our lives but the lives of countless millions of human beings around the world. For you have begun your service in the Congress at an extraordinary moment in history, a moment full of both danger and possibility, a moment in which the United States is the world's premier power, a moment in which we have the opportunity to shape the ground rules for life throughout the post-Cold War world.

Each one of us, as we walk the hallowed halls of the Capitol, must try to reconcile two perhaps antithetical forces: pride and humility. A grand lady and former Member of Congress, Millicent Fenwick of New Jersey, taught me a marvelous quotation, the original source of which I do not know. But hear this: "We proud men pompously compete for nameless graves, while now and then some foundling of fate forgets himself into immortality." That certainly keeps things in the right perspective.

So again, congratulations on what you have accomplished. And thank you for your willingness to serve your country at this extraordinary time in man's ancient quest for peace with freedom, justice, and prosperity. But now, to my second word; and it is a word of caution.

The Congress as a whole is an institution in crisis. It is held in contempt by many Americans. When the people in whose name we legislate—the people who, according to our democratic theory, are the real governors of this land—when they treat the Congress as a joke at best and a pack of scoundrels at worst, then more than our personal egos are at stake.

Democracy itself cannot indefinitely survive public cynicism. Contempt for Congress will inevitably become, over time, contempt for the rule of law. The first task of the new 102nd Congress, then, should be to restore a measure of the people's confidence in their institutions of government. People of good will can and do differ on the roots of today's crisis of confidence in the Congress, and I don't pretend to have even some of the answers. But I would like to reflect with you briefly on two themes which might, over time, help to restore the public's confidence in our institution, if these themes were to become more evident in our work together during the next two years.

The first theme is this: American democracy is a matter of vision and values, not just procedures and rules. During your orientation as new Members you will hear more than you ever wanted to hear about procedures: committee procedures, floor procedures, debating procedures, voting procedures, reporting procedures, and caucus procedures. Rules of procedure are important, especially to the minority. They allow us to conduct our business in something remotely resembling an orderly fashion.

But you must remember, as all of us must, that democracy is not just a matter of procedures. Democracy stands or falls on the strength or weakness of its foundations, the foundations of a democratic *culture*. To put this another way, you cannot have a democracy unless you have enough democrats (spelled with a small "d"). You cannot have a democracy unless you have people who are willing to take up the burden and the glory of self-government. This includes caring enough to inform yourself on the issues and the candidates, and then voting.

You can't have a democracy unless you have people who are willing to acknowledge that the state exists to serve society, and not the other way around.

You can't have democracy unless you have people who are willing to defend the inalienable rights of others—not some others, but all others.

You can't have democracy unless you have people who know that there is a crucial linkage between rights and responsibilities.

And you can't have democracy unless you have people who understand that this democratic experiment of ours is under judgment—the judgment of the principles on which our experiment is based and, I believe, the judgment of God, the ultimate source of the rights so timelessly expressed in our country's birth certificate, the Declaration of Independence.

The brave democrats who led the revolution of 1989 in central and eastern Europe were convinced that democratic politics was impossible without the foundation of the culture of democracy. President Vaclav Havel of Czechoslovakia reminded the Congress earlier this year that the quality of our lives as democrats would determine, over time, the capacity of our political community to serve the common good. In his address to Congress, Havel was drawing from the wellsprings of the western political tradition, which has long taught that democracy requires a virtuous citizenry, a people who understand, as Lord Acton said, that freedom is not a matter of doing what you want, but rather of having the right to do what you ought.

Freedom is vocation and responsibility, duty, civility and order. It is individuality complemented by a humane sociability. Freedom is not license, for license leads to anarchy. Aristotle understood this, as did Jefferson and Madison and Acton, and as does Havel. We must understand it, too.

So yes, procedure is important. But procedure is not what democracy is finally about. Nurturing the culture of democracy is an essential part of our responsibility as United States Representatives.

My second theme is this: There are things worth losing for. This may sound odd, even ironic; for you are here in the flush of victory. And yet it is precisely now that I ask you to contemplate the possibility of defeat—perhaps even the necessity of defeat.

Edmund Burke, in 1774, set forth a model we should all emulate when he told his Bristol constituents: "Your representative owes you, not his industry only, but his judgement, and he betrays instead of serving you if he sacrifices it to your opinion." Let me put the matter plainly: If you are here simply as a tote board registering the current state of opinion in your district, you are not going to serve either your constituents or the Congress well. Your constituents expect you to represent their interests, and that you should certainly do. But you are also a member of the Congress, and your responsibilities are far greater than those of an ombudsman for your district. You must take, at times, a national view, even if, in taking that view, you risk the displeasure of your neighbors and friends back home.

Indeed, I feel obliged to put the matter more sharply still. If you do not know the principle, or the policy, for which you are willing to lose your office, then you are going to do damage here.

This institution needs more Members willing to look beyond the biennial contest for power, more committed to public service as a vocation rather than merely a career. This House needs Members who are at least as clear on the reasons why they would risk losing as they are on the reasons why they wanted to come here in the first place.

On September 2, 1939, the mother of parliaments, the British House of Commons, met to debate whether Great Britain would honor its guarantee to Poland, which had been invaded by Nazi Germany the day before. Prime Minister Chamberlain had made an ineffective and dithering speech to the House, and Arthur Greenwood, spokesman for the Labour Party, got up to respond. "Speaking for the Labour Party," he began, only to be interrupted by an immortal cry from the Conservative back-benches. "Speak for England!" shouted Leo Amery, a former cabinet minister, who is now remembered more for that one call to honor than for anything he did in public office.

"Speak for England," not for party, or for constituents, or for interests, or for re-election, but "for England." Who will speak for America today and in the future? I hope, I pray, that many of you will.

The House needs men and women who will speak for America. There are some here already, in both parties, and you will soon understand who they are. Get to know them, for they are the men and women who make this body an institution worth serving in.

There is no need to romanticize service in the U. S. House of Representatives. But it would be well, at the beginning of your time here, to listen to the echoes of the past that still resonate through this place, if we have the ears to hear them. There are the echoes of Henry Clay and Abraham Lincoln, the echoes of Nicholas Longworth and "Mr. Sam" Rayburn, the echoes of—well, just walk through Statuary Hall and you will know what I mean.

These echoes remind us that great men and women have walked these halls, but that is not a call to nostalgia. There is no reason to think that America's capacity to choose such leaders has ended. The times, indeed, demand a certain greatness from us. Speaking of great leaders, let me leave you with a description and an aspiration in the words of Sir John Colville about the man whom he served for so many years:

"Churchill towers above the rest, less because he was a leader. . . but because he had independence of spirit, the courage of a lion, faith in himself and his cause, the capacity and imagination to inspire, an unwavering belief in the triumph of good over evil, a tireless determination to achieve victory at whatever cost, balanced by chivalry to the foe; and in his soul, the poetry which turned what he was trying to do into romance."

Charles de Gaulle once said, "France would not be true to herself if she were not engaged in some great enterprise." Well, we are all now engaged in a great enterprise. So welcome to the House of Representatives. And if I may leap over the Pyrenees from de Gaulle's France to Spain, vaya con dios!

February 12, 1997

On Term Limits

The popularity of terms limits is a measure of the low esteem our citizens have for politics and for politicians. Of course, the way we who are in office attack each other and demean this institution of which we are parts, it is no wonder we are held in contempt. But before we leap off the cliff, before we vote to amend the Constitution of the United States to impose term limitation upon Members of Congress, we might give some passing deference to our country's Founding Fathers, who, over two hundred years ago, rejected term limits for Congress as they fashioned for us our representative democracy.

I can remember a time when cynicism was considered a pathology, not a fashionable stance, and when it was an honor to be elected to public office. It is true, as it has ever been, that not every public servant has honored his or her office. But to lump together the countless decent ones with those few who betray their trust is unjust, factually wrong, and morally illiterate.

As our nation hurtles forward into an ever more complicated world, how destructive it would be to jettison our most capable leaders when we need their wisdom and judgment so much. Freedom is always in crisis, and America will always have need of its giants, with their enormous experience that gives them both a sense of the past and a vision of the future. To adopt Term Limits, however, is to play Russian roulette with that future, hoping that the years to come will not confront us with dire or deadly situations.

Since it is a constitutional amendment we are asked to adopt today, and to send to the States for their consideration, it is reasonable to ask its proponents just what they seek to accomplish. Well, now it gets a little confusing. One pro-amendment faction insists Congress is too remote, unresponsive, and more interested in reelection than in serving the people, I'll call this the Bob Novak wing, in honor of the distinguished journalist who is, and ever shall be, my good friend. He is also, I believe, one of the most zealous advocates in favor of Term Limits for the reasons stated above.

The other pro-amendment faction argues that Members of Congress are too close to the people, too responsive to them, and insufficiently independent of public opinion polls. I'll call this the George Will wing, in honor of another distinguished journalist, upon whose friendship and counsel, in most matters, I continue to rely. This wing believes that Term Limits will put some needed "constitutional distance" between congressmen and their all too demanding constituents.

Now I must ask: Which is it, a fever or a frostbite? Are we too distant or too close? It appears to me that supporters of this amendment are standing on two stools; and as their arguments drift father apart, they are in danger of getting a constitutional hernia! It seems to me a mighty poor reason to amend our Constitution when its staunchest advocates can't agree on its consequences.

If we adopt one version of this amendment, limiting Members to three two-year terms, enormous super classes would enter the House in six-year cycles. Developing effective leaders under that system would be a roll of the dice. The result would be a revolving door Leadership, with no continuity, no stability, and no historical memory. Just think of the statesmen who would have been lost to America if Term Limits had been in the Constitution: John Quincy Adams, Henry Clay, Arthur Vandenberg, Everett Dirksen, Sam Ervin, Hubert Humphrey, Henry Jackson, Barry Goldwater, Bob Dole, Robert C.Byrd, Bill Natcher, Lee Hamilton. Would our country have survived as free and as strong as it is today without those men and others like them?

Implicit in the argument for Term Limits is the premise that service in Congress is not a particularly difficult job. Scholars say that, two centuries ago, Thomas Jefferson knew everything worth knowing. Whatever one may think of that claim, today it is impossible for anyone to accumulate that store of knowledge. Just think of the range and depth of information and experience needed to deal with just a few of the issues that confront us.

For example, the seemingly obscure issue of electric power deregulation demands mastery of competing commercial interests, the rights of States, environmental safety, anti-trust law, and the day-to-day workings of a $208 billion industry. No easy answers here for newcomers to the Congress! The Superfund reauthorization, always a mare's nest of conflicts and tough choices, demands solutions to problems of litigation, delays, retroactive liability, and the creation of a stable and fair funding stream. An easy task for newcomers? I don't think so.

How about encryption of electronic communications? Or Medicare and Social Security Reform, in the expectation of the Baby Boomers' retirement? How quickly can a newcomer get up to speed on ABM defenses? Or for that matter, China?

I haven't even scratched the surface. This is no place for amateurs. A congressman who makes a career of public service, and who is willing to make the sacrifices that entails, develops a record. That record is a standard of comparison to be judged by. From election to election, he is accountable for the long-term consequences of his actions. No hobbyist legislator, no part-time, lame duck legislator can share that motivation.

Term Limits will encourage early exits from the Congress. Take an attractive job offer when it comes up, because it might not be there when you have to leave. Term Limits will reduce competition for office. Why should a challenger run this year when the seat will be forcibly vacated in two years? A system that does not reward effectiveness or seniority will discourage the most capable individuals, the very people we need.

Term Limits diminishes the opportunities to develop strong ties with your community. That is no virtue. Moreover, it hands off power to the bureaucrats, the lobbyists, the Executive Branch, and the Senate—thus debilitating democracy and radically undercutting the balance of power Mr. Madison devised for the Constitution.

Under Term Limits, this Chamber would be peopled by young

men and women who are starting their careers, plus those few older people who lose nothing by serving a term or two in Congress. Missing from that number would be those in mid-life who would have to give up careers in law or business for a brief fling in public service. But we need them all, the young, the older, and those in the prime of life—the rich and varied mix that makes this truly a House of Representatives.

Whenever we amend the Constitution, we should expand liberty, not diminish or contract it by limiting the voters' right to choose their own representatives. This amendment is not conservative; it is a reaction echo of the 1960's theme, "Don't trust anyone over 30."

The last time the House debated this issue, we who opposed the amendment were accused of arrogance. It was suggested that we thought we were the only ones who are qualified to govern. On the contrary, the beginning of wisdom is to know how much you don't know. If there is any arrogance here, it is among those who, having no idea how difficult it is to draw the line between liberty and order, would deny voters the right to choose whom they will to help draw that line. In a very sad way, this amendment demeans public service as a corrupting influence. It reeks of cynicism and pessimism.

On March 15, 1783, in Newburgh, New York, some officers of the Revolutionary Army met to plot an insurrection. They were furious at an uncaring Continental Congress, which had not paid them or their hungry troops in a long time. Suddenly General Washington arrived and asked leave to address the group. Out of respect for him, they let him speak. At the end, he wanted to read a letter from a Congressman explaining why there were no funds to pay the Army. General Washington searched for his spectacles because he couldn't read the letter. When he found them, he said, "You will permit me to put on my spectacles, for I have grown blind in the service of my country."

Today, there are no General Washingtons among us; but there are a few whose steps have grown slower, and whose sight has grown dimmer, in the service of our country. Their long and faithful service deserves emulation, not oblivion.

The right to vote—and the right to vote for whomever we

please—is the heart and soul of our democracy. If the consent of the governed means anything to you, then your task today is to defend it. Put not your trust in Term Limits. Just trust the people.

September 11, 2006

Valedictory at 'Salute to Henry Hyde'

In the 50 years I've been in politics, and the 32 years I've been privileged to serve in the Congress, I've never lost the conviction that politics is a noble calling—a vocation, not just a job or a career.

Why is politics a vocation? Because, stripped to its essentials, politics isn't about personal power but about common purpose. Politics, as the Greeks understood 2,500 years ago, is an extension of ethics, because politics inevitably touches the question, "How ought we live together?"

That question—to which there are few easy answers—leads to both the exhilaration of politics and to its stresses and burdens. I've had my share of both—the "thrill of victory and the agony of defeat," as Jim McKay used to say on "Wide World of Sports." Still, I remain convinced that the effort demanded of men and women in public life is worth it, because doing the public business by the give-and-take of democratic politics is far superior to all the other ways known to history: tyranny, monarchy, aristocracy. Democratic politics affords all of us the opportunity to exercise our God-given gifts of intellect, judgment, and will to advance the common good. Politics tests our character, time and again. And that constant testing is no bad thing.

That's also why it is essential for good men and women to enter politics. I was once asked to address a class of newly-elected Members of Congress. I think I somewhat startled them by telling them that, while they could do a lot of good in Congress, if they did not know what they were willing to lose their seat for, they were probably going to do some damage, and maybe a lot of damage, down the line. And I continue to hold, however obstinately, to that view: If you don't know the principles on which you're prepared to stand, and lose if necessary, then you shouldn't get into this arena. Because if you don't know what you're willing to lose for, you won't have a clear idea of what's worth fighting for, and why.

All of which, I know, is perhaps a different view of congressional life than what you're likely to find in political science textbooks on congressional government. But I believe it to be true because I believe democracy is much, much more than a matter of settling on the rules by which we sue one another. Democracy isn't a machine that can run by itself. It takes a certain kind of people, living certain virtues, to make the democratic process work, so that the net result is human flourishing, not human degradation.

It takes a certain kind of people, possessed of certain values, to make the democratic process produce "liberty and justice for all." That means that our politics must always attend to the truths, the moral truths, that are the foundation stones of the house of freedom. The truth that there is an inalienable right to life from conception until natural death. The truth that all citizens must be equal before the law. The truth that the laws we pass in Congress stand under the judgment of a higher law, the moral law written on the human heart, and then on tablets of stone.

Let me commend those truths to you again. Thomas Jefferson inscribed them in America's birth certificate, the Declaration of Independence. Abraham Lincoln gave them new resonance amidst the trauma of civil war, and made us more of a nation in the process. And Ronald Reagan brought those truths into world politics and brought down the worst system of tyranny in human history.

As I say goodbye to Washington, I am acutely aware that we live in a time of both extraordinary peril and great opportunity. In these difficult times, I would like to close with a prayer:

Almighty God, we remember that the father of our country knelt in the snow at Valley Forge and asked in humble prayer that he and those who stood with him might never waiver in their dedication to freedom's cause. As you answered Washington's prayer, hear us now. Give us the courage to defend human decency and human dignity. Renew in us our commitment to liberty and justice for all. Give us the unity as a people that will make our cause invincible. Give us the wisdom to know what must be done, and the will and resolve to do it. Grant to us, and to all those of good will, at the end of the struggle that lies before us, a world renewed in justice, in solidarity, and in brotherhood.

My friends, to have been able to stand in the shadow of such giants as Washington, Jefferson, Lincoln and Reagan has been a great privilege. I thank God for that, as I thank God for each of you.

The "Melancholy Procedure"

HJH watches Speaker Newt Gingrich signs the Articles of Impeachment. To his left is Rep. Ed Bryant (R, Tenn.).

T here is a book to be written about the impeachment of
William Jefferson Clinton, but this is not it. What follows
this brief introduction is, instead, a compendium of the key
speeches I had to make during what I called at the time "this melancholy procedure." That entire chapter in the history of the American
presidency appears in hindsight like the conflation of an off-color
sit-com with a Shakespearean tragedy. To future historians who
write textbooks for young students, it will present unique difficulties in the explanation of human behavior.

Perhaps the materials which follow this introduction will assist
them. I hope so; for in my formal remarks as the chief
Impeachment Trial Manager for the House of Representatives, I
always attempted to keep the public focus, not on tangential issues
of all too personal conduct, but on the heart of the matter: Whether
the chief executive of the United States had willfully committed
perjury and, therefore, had subjected himself to the punitive provisions of the Constitution we were all sworn to uphold.

That's not racy stuff, but Heaven knows the country had had
more than enough titillation over Mr. Clinton's antics, confirmed or
alleged, in the years leading up to his impeachment. One of the persistent criticisms directed at the impeachment managers is that we
released too much prurient material, all to embarrass the President,
that was unnecessary for the prosecution. But we did not seek to
release that material (about 50 boxes of transcripts and exhibits).
We were urged to do so by prominent Democrats, including
Representatives John Dingell and Dick Gephardt, who feared we
would release only the most damaging information and not any
exculpatory documents. They demanded we make it all public, and
so we did.

The Democrats' strategy throughout the ordeal was to shift
focus from the perjury and obstruction charges to the alleged sexu-

al misconduct and thus characterize the prosecution as a bunch of right-wing blue-noses who were persecuting an errant but benign president for their own base political reasons. This was what the major media wanted to believe, and so it became doctrine—and still is today. (Which brings to mind a line from James J. Kilpatrick's column of many years ago: "Falsehood flies on falcon's wings while Truth shuffles along in wooden shoes.")

For better or worse, the impeachment proceedings of 1998-99 are likely to cast a shadow over this country's politics for the immediate future. The reason should be obvious: Hillary Clinton's presidential candidacy and her husband's prominent involvement in it. Like it or not, she cannot escape the turnabout of that famous line she uttered when the Clintons were first campaigning for the White House: "If you elect him, you get me." Switch around the pronouns and, fairly or not, you have what is sure to be an important issue in the 2008 race.

That may not be fair to Mrs. Clinton, but fairness is often in short supply in contemporary politics. I knew that, as did every Member of the House of Representatives who voted for impeachment. We knew we were directly taking on the most effective and ruthless network of political operators, media lords, and academic hangers-on this country has seen since the heyday of the Kennedy machine. But it wasn't as if we had any choice in the matter.

Though impeachment may be a rare procedure, it is a clearly established one, prescribed by our Constitution with little leeway for interpretation. Once evidence of high crimes and misdemeanors has been presented to the House of Representatives, certain procedures are to be followed more or less automatically. Such had been the case, only a few years before the Clinton affair, with regard to two federal judges, both appointees of President Carter, who were duly impeached by the House and, after trial before the Senate, convicted and removed from office. (One of them is now a Member of the House of Representatives, the same body which had earlier sent him to the Senate for trial.) Though federal judges are important figures, there is, of course, far greater moment in the impeachment of a president. Even so, the process is the same for both the high and the highest. Chief Justice William Rehnquist's tome, *Grand Inquests*, about the impeachment trials of Justice Samuel Chase and President Andrew Johnson, explains that process in authoritative detail, sparing me the necessity for repeating it here.

Within that context, we Members of the House had little choice but to take up the question of impeachment. In brute political terms, none of us, of either party, had any reason to want Vice President Al Gore to assume the presidency, just in time to run as an advantaged incumbent in the 2000 election. Moreover, entirely apart from political considerations, I would guess that most of my colleagues at the time just wished we could close up the doors and windows of the White House, turn off the cameras, and let the residents there work out whatever marital problems had so abruptly come to the attention of a startled national audience. Anyone who has ever had to confront his own misdeeds, and put back together relationships fractured by his own misconduct, had to know how difficult that is, even in private. With the whole world watching, it's almost impossible.

If only Bill Clinton hadn't lied. If only he had not committed perjury in the course of a federal investigation, there would have been no legal consequences to his conduct, and the Congress would have had no business butting into the matter. But his perjury was an act against the state by the head of state, a repudiation of government by the head of government, a deliberate show of contempt for his oath of office and the Constitution on which his office rests. That's not a technical offense.

To those Americans—and I realize there are tens of millions of them—who believe the Republican-controlled Congress unfairly persecuted President Clinton, I can only ask, what else were we supposed to do? Some, on both sides of the partisan aisle, proposed a resolution of censure. For certain Democrats, this was an easy way out. They could chastise their President without alienating his hard-core supporters in their party. It was virtue on the cheap. For many Republicans, astounded that Mr. Clinton was going to appear vindicated, censure seemed to offer at least the illusion that justice had prevailed.

After much agonizing, I concluded I could never accept censure. It is a procedure not known in our laws and alien to our Constitution. It was far preferable for a guilty president to escape punishment altogether rather than establish the terrible precedent of congressional censure of the chief executive—any chief executive at any time. We could not allow certain Senators to either salve their conscience or placate their constituents by that innovation. For once it was wielded against a president, it would surely be employed again and again by congressional majorities hostile to his successors.

The only other option was resignation. There was a brief period, lasting no more than 48 hours, when much of official Washington and its "chattering class" of talking media heads believed that the President would spare himself and his country the ordeal of impeachment by resigning. The more jaded souls among us scoffed at that prospect, and we were right. The Left never walks away from power and never puts the national interest ahead of its liberal agenda. During the initial parts of the impeachment process, I kept hoping that a few of the most prominent Democrats, either Senators or national party leaders, would break ranks and demand a resignation. By an intervention like that, back in 1974, Senator Barry Goldwater and other senior Republican senators privately told President Nixon, in more diplomatic terms, that the jig was up and he should hit the road. But I was disappointed. As long as Bill Clinton defiantly held the presidency, he could count on his PR machinery, the loyalty of most rank and file Democrats, and the trappings of world responsibility—while his congressional adversaries would seem a bunch of prissy moralists. As long as the Clintons remained in the White House, he could count on generous contributions to his legal defense, anticipate huge future earnings, and maintain his wife's viability as a future candidate in her own right.

Most of all, he could count on Senate Democrats, or at least enough of them to block his conviction. (A supermajority of two-thirds of those present and voting, or 66 of the 100 senators, was required for conviction.) As it turned out, he was able to count on all the Democratic senators, every last one of them voting "not guilty," in addition to Pennsylvania's Republican Senator Arlen Specter, who offered what he called a "Scottish verdict," neither "guilty" nor "not guilty," simply "not proven."

For a defendant, that lineup was five aces in the hole. It's what we might call the O.J. Simpson doctrine: Let the prosecutor do his worst, as long as you own the jury. No matter how rough the road ahead, you know it leads to the winner's circle. A good prosecutor knows that too, knows when even his tightest case, with the most solid evidence, is going to lose because of a jury problem. So what do you do? You do your duty.

A criminal act demands a criminal trial, and in that proceeding the prosecution (that would be me) must ignore the defendant's earlier record and present evidence only about the specific charge. Sure, there were Members of Congress—and a large portion of the public—who were convinced that the President had long been guilty of all sorts of wrong-doing, whether financial or political or moral; but that was irrelevant. An individual accused of shoplifting may also be a tax fraud and a wife-beater, but that isn't the proper concern of either the prosecutor or the jury. Nor was it our business, in the House of Representatives, to evaluate Mr. Clinton's character, associates, or business dealings.

Knowing how the Clinton team played politics, always sliding into home with their spikes aimed at your face, we expected the blows to come. I was not at all surprised when the President's defenders reached four decades back into the past to hurt me and my family as much as they could. After all, they were committed activists of the ideological Left, no different from the extremists who, at one point, had me followed to church in order to prove that I was getting my marching orders from the Vatican. In 1993, when a North Carolina abortionist wrote the White House a letter attacking me for being "paid off by the Catholic church," George Stephanopoulos—yes, the genial guy who now poses as a newsman on ABC—actually circulated the guy's policy suggestions to the White House senior staff. Even so, hardened as I was to such tactics, I was shocked when three members of my staff had their car tires slashed in the House parking garage. I still wonder whether the unexplained fire at the Irish pub owned by my chief of staff in nearby Alexandria, Virginia, was arson. And to this day, neither Conan O'Brien nor the network that carries his late-night show has ever apologized for broadcasting the diatribe of a particularly malignant Hollywood actor, who on the air expressed the wish that I and my family might be stoned by the public.

Through it all, none of us blinked. My staff, fully aware of the historic magnitude of their work, was more than equal to it. My fellow House managers made me feel like Henry V at Agincourt, a member of their band of brothers. As long as God grants me memory, I will recall this litany of honor: Sensenbrenner, Bryant, Hutchinson, Rogan, McCollum, Gekas, Barr, Cannon, Chabot, Canady, Graham, Buyer. They bring to mind John Greenleaf Whittier's account of Abraham Davenport, in a virtually forgotten poem by that name. It opens with a witticism with which I do not entirely agree:

> *In the old days (a custom laid aside*
> *With breeches and cocked hats) the people sent*
> *Their wisest men to make the public laws.*

Davenport was one of them, a member of the Connecticut legislature in the month of May, 1780, when, according to Whittier's imaginative account, a solar eclipse seemed to augur the Second Coming. Davenport's colleagues called for immediate adjournment, but he was unmoved, declaring:

> *This well may be*
> *The Day of Judgment which the world awaits;*
> *But be it so or not, I only know*
> *My present duty, and my Lord's command*
> *To occupy till he come. So at the post*
> *Where He hath set me in His providence,*
> *I choose, for one, to meet him face to face—*
> *No faithless servant frightened from my task,*
> *But ready when the Lord of the harvest calls;*

And therefore, with all reverence, I would say,
Let God do his work, we will see to ours.
Bring in the candles.

Whereupon the lawmakers continued their deliberations, all the while awaiting the crack of doom. Of course, it did not come, but what Whittier concluded about Abraham Davenport can equally be applied to those Members of the House who stood by my side in the impeachment Day of Judgment. To me, they will always remain

A witness to the ages as they pass
That simple duty hath no place for fear.

December 18, 1998

House Speech on Impeachment

Mr. Speaker, my colleagues of the people's House, I wish to talk to you about the rule of law. After months of argument, hours of debate, there is no need for further complexity. The question before this House is rather simple. It's not a question of sex. Sexual misconduct and adultery are private acts and are none of Congress' business.

It's not even a question of lying about sex. The matter before the House is a question of lying under oath. This is a public act, not a private act. This is called perjury. The matter before the House is a question of the willful, premeditated, deliberate corruption of the nation's system of justice. Perjury and obstruction of justice cannot be reconciled with the office of the president of the United States.

The personal fate of the president is not the issue. The political fate of his party is not the issue. The Dow Jones Industrial Average is not the issue. The issue is perjury—lying under oath. The issue is obstruction of justice, which the president has sworn the most solemn oath to uphold.

That oath constituted a compact between the president and the American people. That compact has been broken. The people's trust has been betrayed. The nation's chief executive has shown himself unwilling or incapable of enforcing its laws, for he has corrupted the rule of law—the rule of law—by his perjury and his obstruction of justice.

That and nothing other than that is the issue before this house.

We have heard ceaselessly that, even if the president is guilty of the charges in the Starr referral, they don't rise to the level of an impeachable offense.

Well, just what is an impeachable offense?

One authority, Professor Stephen Presser of Northwestern University Law School said, and I quote, "Impeachable offenses are those which demonstrate a fundamental betrayal of public trust. They suggest the federal official has deliberately failed in his duty to uphold the Constitution and laws he was sworn to enforce." Close quote.

And so we must decide if a president, the chief law enforcement officer of the land, the person who appoints the attorney general, the person who nominates every federal judge, the person who nominates to the Supreme Court and the only person with a constitutional obligation to take care that the laws be faithfully executed, can lie under oath repeatedly and maintain it is not a breach of trust sufficient for impeachment.

The president is the trustee of the nation's conscience and so are we here today. There have been many explosions in our committee hearings on the respective role of the House and Senate. Under the Constitution, the House accuses and the Senate adjudicates.

True, the formula language of our articles recites the ultimate goal of removal from office, but this language doesn't trump the Constitution, which defines the separate functions, the different functions, of the House and the Senate.

Our Founding Fathers didn't want the body that accuses to be the same one that renders final judgment, and they set up an additional safeguard of a two-thirds vote for removal. So despite protests, our job is to decide if there is enough evidence to submit to the Senate for a trial.

That's what the Constitution says, no matter what the president's defenders say. When Ben Franklin, on September 18, 1787, told a Mrs. Powell, that the founders and framers had given us a republic if you can keep it, perhaps he anticipated a future time when bedrock principles of our democracy would be mortally threatened as the rule of law stands in the line of fire today.

Nothing I can think of more clearly illustrates that America is a continuing experiment—never finished—that our democracy is always a work in progress than this debate today—for we sit here with the power to shake and reconfigure the charter of our freedom, just as the founders and framers did. We can strengthen our Constitution by giving it content and meaning, or we can weaken and wound it by tolerating and thus encouraging lies under oath and evasions and breaches of trust on the part of our chief executive.

The president's defenders in this House have rarely denied the facts. They have not seriously challenged the contention of the independent counsel that the president did not tell the truth in two sworn testimonies. They have not seriously attempted to discredit the facts brought before the committee by the independent counsel. They've admitted, in effect, he did it. But then they've argued that this does not rise to the level of an impeachable offense.

This is the "so-what" defense, whereby a chief executive, the successor to George Washington, can cheapen the oath, and it really doesn't matter.

They suggest that to impeach the president is to reverse the result of national election, as though Senator Dole would become president.

They propose novel remedies like a congressional censure that may appease some constituents and certainly mollify the press but, in my judgment, betray a lack of seriousness about the Constitution, the separation of powers and the carefully balanced relationship of checks and balances between Congress and the president that was wisely crafted by the framers.

A resolution of censure, to mean anything, must punish if only to tarnish his reputation. But we have no authority under the Constitution to punish the president. It's called separation of powers.

As you know, we've been attacked for not producing fact witnesses. But this is the first impeachment inquiry in history with the Office of Independent Counsel in place, and their referral to us consisted of 60,000 pages of sworn testimony, grand jury transcripts, depositions, statements, affidavits, video and audio tapes.

We had the facts and we had them under oath.

We had Ms. Lewinsky's heavily corroborated testimony under a grant of immunity that would be revoked if she lied.

We accepted that and so did they. Else why didn't they call any others whose credibility they questioned as their own witnesses? No, there was so little dispute on the facts, they called no fact witnesses and have even based a resolution of censure on the same facts.

Let us be clear. The vote that all of us are asked to cast is, in the final analysis, a vote on the rule of law.

Now the rule of law is one of the great achievements of our civilization, for the alternative is the rule of raw power. We here today are the heirs of 3,000 years of history in which humanity slowly, painfully, at great cost evolved a form of politics in which law, not brute force, is the arbiter of our public destinies.

We are the heirs of the Ten Commandments and the Mosaic Law, a moral code for a free people, who, having been liberated from bondage, sought in law a means to avoid falling back into the habits of slaves.

We are the heirs of Roman Law, the first legal system by which peoples of different cultures, languages, races and religions came to live together in a form of political community.

We are the heirs of the Magna Carta, by which the free men of England began to break the arbitrary and unchecked power of royal absolutism. We're the heirs of a long tradition of parliamentary development in which the rule of law gradually came to replace royal prerogative as a means for governing a society of free men and women.

We're the heirs of 1776 and of an epic moment in human affairs, when the founders of this Republic pledged their lives, their fortunes and their sacred honors—think of that: sacred honor—to the defense of the rule of law.

We are the heirs of a hard-fought war between the states, which vindicated the rule of law over the appetites of some for owning others. We are the heirs of the 20th century's great struggles against totalitarianism, in which the rule of law was defended at immense cost against the worst tyrannies in human history.

The phrase "rule of law" is no pious aspiration from a civics textbook. The rule of law is what stands between all of us and the arbitrary exercise of power by the state. The rule of law is the safeguard of our liberties. The rule of law is what allows us to live our freedom in ways that honor the freedom of others, while strengthening the common good.

The rule of law is like a three-legged stool. One leg is an honest judge, the second leg is an ethical bar, and the third is an enforceable oath. All three are indispensable to avoid political collapse.

In 1838, Abraham Lincoln celebrated the rule of law before the Young Men's Lyceum of Springfield, Illinois, and linked it to the perpetuation of American liberties and American political institutions. Listen to Lincoln, from 1838:

"Let every American, every lover of liberty, every well-wisher to his posterity, swear by the blood of the revolution never to violate in the least particular the laws of the country; and never to tolerate their violation by others. As the patriots of '76 did to support the Declaration of Independence, so to the support of the Constitution and laws, let every American pledge his life, his property and his sacred honor. Let every man remember that to violate the law is to trample on the blood of his father and to tear the character of his own and his children's liberty. Let reverence for the laws be breathed by every American mother to the lisping babe that prattles on her lap. Let it be taught in the schools, seminaries, colleges. Let it be written in primers, spelling books, almanacs. Let it be preached from the pulpit, proclaimed in legislative halls and enforced in the courts of justice."

So said Lincoln.

My colleagues, we have been sent here to strengthen and defend the rule of law—not to weaken, not to attenuate it, not to disfigure it. This is not a question of perfection; it's a question of foundations.

This isn't a matter of setting the bar too high; it's a matter of securing the basic structure of our freedom—which is the rule of law.

No man or woman, no matter how highly placed, no matter how effective a communicator, no matter how gifted a manipulator of opinion or winner of votes, can be above the law in a democracy. That is not a counsel of perfection. That is a rock-bottom, irreducible principle of our public life.

There's no avoiding the issue before us, much as I wish we could. We are, in one way or another, establishing the parameters of permissible presidential conduct.

In creating a presidential system, the framers invested that office with extraordinary powers. If those powers are not exercised within the boundaries of the rule of law, if the president breaks the law by perjury and obstructs justice by willfully corrupting the legal system, that president must be removed from office.

We cannot have one law for the ruler and another law for the ruled. This was once broadly understood in our land. If that understanding is lost or if it becomes seriously eroded, the American democratic experiment and the freedom it guarantees is in jeopardy. That and not the fate of one man, or one political party, or one electoral cycle is what we're being asked to vote on today.

In casting our votes we should look not simply to ourselves, but to the past and to the future. Let's look back to Bunker Hill, Concord, Lexington. Let's look across the river to Arlington Cemetery where American heroes who gave their lives for the sake of the rule of law lie buried. And let us not betray their memory.

Let's look to the future, to the children of today who are the presidents and members of Congress of the next century. And let's not crush their hope that they too will inherit a law-governed society.

Let's declare unmistakably that perjury and obstruction of justice disqualify a man from retaining the presidency of the United States.

There is a mountain of details which are assembled in a coherent mosaic in the committee report. It reads like a novel, only it's non-fiction. It really happened. And the corroboration is compelling. Read the report and be convinced.

What we're telling you today are not the ravings of some vindictive political crusade but a reaffirmation of a set of values that are tarnished and dim these days, but it is given to us to restore them so our founding fathers would be proud.

Listen, it's your country. The president is our flag bearer.

He stands out in front of our people when the flag is flowing. Catch the falling flag as we keep our appointment with history.

January 14, 1999

Impeachment Trial: Opening Remarks

M r. Chief Justice and Members of the Senate. We are brought together on this most solemn and historic occasion to perform important duties assigned to us by the Constitution.

We want you to know how much we respect you and this institution and how grateful we are for your guidance and cooperation.

With your permission, we the managers of the House are here to set forth the evidence in support of two articles of impeachment against President William Jefferson Clinton. You are here seated in this historic chamber not to embark on some great legislative debate, which these stately walls have so often witnessed, but to listen to the evidence, as those who must sit in judgment.

To guide you in this grave duty you have taken an oath of impartiality. With the simple words "I do," you have pledged to put aside personal bias and partisan interest and to do "impartial justice." Your willingness to take up this calling has once again reminded the world of the unique brilliance of America's constitutional system of government. We are here, Mr. Chief Justice and Distinguished Senators, as advocates for the Rule of Law, for Equal Justice Under the Law and for the sanctity of the oath.

The oath. In many ways the case you will consider in the coming days is about those two words "I do," pronounced at two Presidential inaugurations by a person whose spoken words have singular importance to our nation and to the great globe itself.

More than four hundred fifty years ago, Sir Thomas More, former Lord Chancellor of England, was imprisoned in the Tower of London because he had, in the name of conscience, defied the absolute power of the King. As the playwright Robert Bolt tells it, More was visited by his family, who tried to persuade him to speak the words of the oath that would save his life, even while, in his mind and heart, he held firm to his conviction that the King was in error. More refused. As he told his daughter, Margaret, "When a man takes an oath, Meg, he's holding his own self in his hands. Like water. And if he opens his fingers then—he needn't hope to find himself again . . ." Sir Thomas More, the most brilliant lawyer of his generation, a scholar with an international reputation, the center of a warm and affectionate family life which he cherished, went to his death rather than take an oath in vain.

Members of the Senate, what you do over the next few weeks will forever affect the meaning of those two words "I do." You are now stewards of the oath. It's significance in public service and our cherished system of justice will never be the same after this. Depending on what you decide, it will either be strengthened in its power to achieve Justice or it will go the way of so much of our moral infrastructure and become a mere convention, full of sound and fury, signifying nothing.

The House of Representatives has named myself and twelve other Members as Managers of its case. I have the honor of introducing those distinguished Members and explaining how we will make our initial presentation. The gentleman from Wisconsin, Representative Jim Sensenbrenner, will begin the presentation with an overview of the case. Representative Sensenbrenner is the

Ranking Republican Member of the House Judiciary Committee, and has served for twenty years. In 1989, Representative Sensenbrenner was a House Manager in the impeachment trial of Judge Walter L. Nixon who was convicted on two articles of impeachment for making false and misleading statements before a federal grand jury.

Following Representative Sensenbrenner will be a team of Managers who will make a presentation of the relevant facts of this case. From the very outset of this ordeal, there has been a great deal of speculation and misinformation about the facts. That has been unfortunate for everyone involved. We believe that a full presentation of the facts and the law by the House Managers—will be most helpful.

Representative Ed Bryant from Tennessee was the United States Attorney from the Western District of Tennessee. As a Captain in the Army, Representative Bryant served in the Judge Advocate General Corps and taught at the United States Military Academy at West Point. Representative Bryant will explain the background of the events that led to the illegal actions of the President. Following Representative Bryant, Representative Asa Hutchinson from Arkansas will give a presentation of the factual basis for Article II, obstruction of justice. Representative Hutchinson is a former United States Attorney for the Western District of Arkansas. Next, you will hear from Representative Jim Rogan from California. Representative Rogan is a former California state judge and Los Angeles County Deputy District Attorney. Representative Rogan will give a presentation of the factual basis for Article I, grand jury perjury. This should conclude our presentation for today.

Tomorrow, Representative Bill McCollum of Florida will tie all of the facts together and give a factual summation. Representative McCollum is the Chairman of the Subcommittee on Crime and is a former Naval Reserve Commander and member of the Judge Advocate General Corps.

Following the presentation of the facts, a team of managers will present the law of perjury and the law of obstruction of justice and how it applies to the articles of impeachment before you. While the

Senate has made it clear that a crime is not essential to impeachment and removal from office, these Managers will explain how egregious and criminal the conduct alleged in the articles of impeachment is. This team includes Representative George Gekas of Pennsylvania, Representative Steve Chabot of Ohio, Representative Bob Barr of Georgia and Representative Chris Cannon of Utah. Representative Gekas is the Chairman of the Subcommittee on Commercial and Administrative Law. In 1989, Representative Gekas served as a Manager of the impeachment trial of Judge Alcee Hastings whom the Senate convicted on eight articles for making false and misleading statements under oath and one article of conspiracy to engage in a bribery. Representative Gekas is a former assistant district attorney. Representative Chabot serves on the Subcommittee on Crime and has experience as a criminal defense lawyer. Representative Barr is a former United States Attorney for the Northern District of Georgia, where he specialized in public corruption; he also has experience as a criminal defense attorney. Representative Cannon has had experience as the Deputy Associate Solicitor General of the Department of the Interior and as a practicing attorney. That should conclude our presentation for Friday.

On Saturday, three Managers will make a presentation on Constitutional law as it relates to this case. There has been a great deal of argument about whether the conduct alleged in the articles rises to the level of removable offenses. This team's analysis of the precedents of the Senate and application of the facts of this case will make it clear that the Senate has established the conduct alleged in the articles to be removable offenses. In this presentation you will hear from Representative Charles Canady of Florida, Representative Steve Buyer of Indiana and Representative Lindsey Graham of South Carolina. Representative Canady is the Chairman of the Subcommittee on the Constitution and one of the leading voices on constitutional law in the House of Representatives. Representative Buyer served in the United States Army as a member of the Judge Advocate General Corps where he was assigned as Special Assistant to the United States Attorney in Virginia. He also served as a Deputy to the Indiana Attorney General. Representative Graham served in the Air Force as a member of the Judge Advocate General Corps and as a South Carolina Assistant Attorney.

Following the presentation of the facts, the law of perjury and obstruction of justice and constitutional law, we will give you a final summation and closing to our initial presentation.

January 16, 1999

Impeachment Trial: Closing Remarks

M
r. Chief Justice, Counsel for the President and Distinguished Members of the Senate: One of the most memorable aspects of this proceeding was the solemn occasion wherein every Senator in this chamber took an oath to do impartial justice under the Constitution.

The President of the United States took an oath to tell the truth in his testimony before the grand jury, just as he had, on two prior occasions, sworn a solemn oath to preserve, protect and defend the Constitution and to "faithfully execute the laws of the United States."

Despite massive and relentless efforts to change the subject, the case before you Senators is not about sexual misconduct or adultery—those are private acts and none of our business.

It is not even a question of lying about sex.

The matter before this body is a question of lying under oath. This is a public act.

The matter before you is a question of the willful, premeditated, deliberate corruption of the nation's system of justice, through Perjury and Obstruction of Justice. These are public acts, and when committed by the chief law enforcement officer of the land, the one who appoints the Attorney General and nominates the Judiciary—these do become the concern of Congress.

That is why your judgment should rise above politics, above partisanship, above polling data. This case is a test of whether what the Founding Fathers described as "sacred honor" still has meaning in our time: two hundred twenty-two years after those two words—sacred honor—were inscribed in our country's birth certificate, our charter of freedom, our Declaration of Independence.

Every school child in the United States has an intuitive sense of the "sacred honor" that is one of the foundation stones of the American house of freedom. For every day, in every classroom in America, our children and grandchildren pledge allegiance to a nation, "under God." That statement, that America is "one nation under God," is not a prideful or arrogant claim. It is a statement of humility: all of us, as individuals, stand under the judgment of God, or the transcendent truths by which we hope, finally, to be judged.

So does our country.

The Presidency is an office of trust. Every public office is a public trust, but the Office of President is a very special public trust. The President is the trustee of the national conscience. No one owns the office of President, the people do. The President is elected by the people and their representatives in the electoral college. And in accepting the burdens of that great office, the President, in his inaugural oath, enters into a covenant—a binding agreement of mutual trust and obligation—with the American people.

Shortly after his election and during his first months in office, President Clinton spoke with some frequency about a "new covenant" in America. In this instance, let us take the President at his word: that his office is a covenant—a solemn pact of mutual trust and obligation—with the American people. Let us take the President seriously when he speaks of covenants: because a covenant is about promise-making and promise-keeping.

For it is because the President has defaulted on the promises he made—it is because he has violated the oaths he has sworn—that he has been impeached.

The debate about impeachment during the Constitutional Convention of 1787 makes it clear that the Framers of the Constitution regarded impeachment and removal from office on conviction as a remedy for a fundamental betrayal of trust by the President. The Framers had invested the presidential office with great powers. They knew that those powers could be—and would be—abused if any President were to violate, in a fundamental way, the oath he had sworn to faithfully execute the nation's laws.

For if the President did so violate his oath of office, the covenant of trust between himself and the American people would be broken.

Today, we see something else: that the fundamental trust between America and the world can be broken, if a presidential per-jurer represents our country in world affairs. If the President calcu-latedly and repeatedly violates his oath, if the President breaks the covenant of trust he has made with the American people, he can no longer be trusted. And, because the executive plays so large a role in representing the country to the world, America can no longer be trusted.

It is often said that we live in an age of increasing interdepen-dence. If that is true, and the evidence for it is all around us, then the future will require an even stronger bond of trust between the President and the nation: because with increasing interdependence comes an increased necessity of trust.

This is one of the basic lessons of life. Parents and children know this. Husbands and wives know it. Teachers and students know it, as do doctors and patients, suppliers and customers, lawyers and clients, clergy and parishioners: the greater the inter-dependence, the greater the necessity of trust; the greater the inter-dependence, the greater the imperative of promise-keeping.

Trust, not what James Madison called the "parchment barriers" of laws, is the fundamental bond between the people and their elected representatives, between those who govern and those who are governed. Trust is the mortar that secures the foundations of the American house of freedom. And the Senate of the United States, sitting in judgment in this impeachment trial, should not ignore, or minimize, or dismiss the fact that the bond of trust has been broken, because the President has violated both his oaths of office and the oath he took before his grand jury testimony.

In recent months, it has often been asked—it has too often been asked—so what? What is the harm done by this lying under oath, by this perjury?

I think the answer would have been clear to those who once pledged their sacred honor to the cause of liberty.

The answer would have been clear to those who crafted the world's most enduring written constitution.

No greater harm can be done than breaking the covenant of trust between the President and the people; between the three branches of our government; and between the country and the world.

For to break that covenant of trust is to dissolve the mortar that binds the foundation stones of our freedom into a secure and solid edifice. And to break that covenant of trust by violating one's oath is to do grave damage to the rule of law among us.

That none of us is above the law is a bedrock principle of democracy. To erode that bedrock is to risk even further injustice. To erode that bedrock is to subscribe to a "divine right of kings" theory of governance, in which those who govern are absolved from adhering to the basic moral standards to which the governed are accountable.

We must never tolerate one law for the Ruler and another for the Ruled. If we do, we break faith with our ancestors from Bunker Hill, Lexington and Concord to Flanders Field, Normandy, Iwo Jima, Panmunjon, Saigon and Desert Storm. . . .

Lying under oath is an abuse of freedom. Obstruction of Justice is a degradation of law. There are people in prison for just such offenses. What in the world do we say to them about Equal Justice if we overlook this conduct in the President?

Some may say, as many have said in recent months, that this is to pitch the matter too high. The President's lie, it is said, was about a "trivial matter;" it was a lie to spare embarrassment about misconduct on a "private occasion."

The confusing of what is essentially a private matter, and none of our business, with lying under oath to a court and a grand jury has been only one of the distractions we have had to deal with.

Senators: as men and women with a serious experience of public affairs, we can all imagine a situation in which a President might shade the truth when a great issue of the national interest or the national security was at stake. We have all been over that terrain. We know the thin ice on which any of us skates when blurring the edges of the truth for what we consider a compelling, demanding public purpose.

Morally serious men and women can imagine circumstances, at the far edge of the morally permissible, when, with the gravest matters of national interest at stake, a President could shade the truth in order to serve the common good. But under oath . . . for a private pleasure?

In doing this, the Office of President of the United States has been debased . . . and the Justice System jeopardized.

In doing this, he has broken his covenant of trust with the American people.

The Framers of the Constitution also knew that the Office of President of the United States could be gravely damaged if it continued to be unworthily occupied. That is why they devised the process of impeachment by the House and trial by the Senate. It is, in truth, a direct process.

If, on impeachment, the President is convicted, he is removed from office—and the Office itself suffers no permanent damage. If, on impeachment, the President is acquitted, the issue is resolved once and for all, and the Office is similarly protected from permanent damage.

But if, on impeachment, the President is not convicted and removed from office despite the fact that numerous Senators are convinced that he has, in the words of one proposed resolution of censure, "egregiously failed" the test of his oath of office, "violated the trust of the American people," and "dishonored the office which they entrusted to him," then the Office of the Presidency has been deeply, and perhaps permanently, damaged.

And that is a further reason why President Clinton must be convicted of the charges brought before you by the House of Representatives, and removed from office. To fail to do so, while conceding that the President has engaged in egregious and dishonorable behavior that has broken the covenant of trust between himself and the American people, is to diminish the office of President of the United States in an unprecedented and unacceptable way.

Senators: please permit me a word on my own behalf and on behalf of my colleagues of the House. It is necessary to clarify an important point.

None of us comes to this chamber today without a profound sense of our own responsibilities in life, and of the many ways in which we have failed to meet those responsibilities, to one degree or another. None of us comes before you claiming to be a perfect man or a perfect citizen, just as none of you imagines yourself perfect. All of us, members of the House and Senate, know that we come to this difficult task as flawed human beings, under judgment.

That is the way of this world: flawed human beings must, according to the rule of law, judge other flawed human beings.

But the issue before the Senate of the United States is not the question of its own members' personal moral condition. Nor is the issue before the Senate the question of the personal moral condition of the members of the House of Representatives. The issue here is whether the President of the United States has violated the rule of law and thereby broken his covenant of trust with the American people. This is a public issue, involving the gravest matter of the public interest. And it is not affected, one way or another, by the personal moral condition of any member of either house of Congress, or by whatever expressions of personal chagrin the President has managed to express.

Senators: we of the House do not come before you today lightly. And, if you will permit me, it is a disservice to the House to suggest that it has brought these articles of impeachment before you in a frivolous, mean-spirited, or irresponsible way. That is not true.

We have brought these articles of impeachment because we are convinced, in conscience, that the President of the United States lied under oath: that the President committed perjury on several occasions before a Federal grand jury. We have brought these articles of impeachment because we are convinced, in conscience, that the President willfully obstructed justice, and thereby threatened the legal system he swore a solemn oath to protect and defend.

These are not trivial matters. These are not partisan matters. These are matters of justice, the justice that each of you has taken a solemn oath to serve in this trial.

Some of us have been called "Clinton-haters." I must tell you, distinguished Senators, that this impeachment is not, for those of us from the House, a question of hating anyone. This is not a question of who we hate, this is a question of what we love: and among the things we love are the rule of law, equal justice before the law, and honor in our public life. All of us are trying as hard as we can to do our duty as we see it . . . no more and no less.

Senators: This trial is being watched around the world. Some of those watching, thinking themselves superior in their cynicism, wonder what it is all about. But others know.

Political prisoners know that this is about the rule of law—the great alternative to arbitrary and unchecked state power.

The families of executed dissidents know that this is about the rule of law—the great alternative to the lethal abuse of power by the state.

Those yearning for freedom know that this is about the rule of law—the hard-won structure by which men and women can live by their God-given dignity and secure their God-given rights in ways that serve the common good.

If they know this, can we not know it?

If, across the river in Arlington Cemetery, there are American heroes who died in defense of the rule of law, can we give less than the full measure of our devotion to that great cause?

I have received a letter last week that expresses my feelings far better than my poor words.

> Dear Chairman Hyde, my name is William Preston Summers. How are you doing? I am a third grader in room 504 at Chase Elementary School in Chicago.
>
> I'm writing this letter because I have something to tell you. I have thought of a punishment for the president of the United States of America. The punishment should be that he should write a 100-word essay by hand. I have to write an essay when I lie.
>
> It is bad to lie because it just gets you in more trouble. I hate getting in trouble. It's just like the boy who cried 'wolf' and the wolf ate the boy. It is important to tell the truth.
>
> I like to tell the truth because it gets you in less trouble. If you do not tell the truth, people do not believe you. It is important to believe the president because he is a important person. If you cannot believe the president, who can you believe? If you have no one to believe in, then how do you run your life?
>
> I do not believe the president tells the truth any more right now. After he writes the essay and tells the truth, I will believe him again. (signed) William Summers.

Then there's a P.S. from his dad: "Dear Representative Hyde, I made my son William either write you a letter or an essay as a punishment for lying. Part of his defense for his lying was that the president lied. He's still having difficulty understanding why the president can lie and not be punished."

Mr. Chief Justice and Senators, on June 6, 1994, the 50th anniversary of the American landing on the beaches of Normandy, I stood among the field of white crosses and Stars of David. The British had a military band of bagpipes playing Amazing Grace. I walked up to one cross to read a name, but there was none. All it said was "Here lies in Honored Glory a Comrade in Arms Known but to God."

How do we keep the faith with that comrade in arms? Go to the Vietnam Memorial on the National Mall and press your hands against some of the 58,000 names carved in the wall—and ask

yourself how we can redeem the debt we owe all those who pur-
chased our freedom with their lives.

How do we keep faith with them?

I think I know how; we work to make this country the kind of
America they were willing to die for. That's an America where the
idea of sacred honor still has the power to stir men's souls.

I hope that a hundred years from today, people will look back
at what we have done and say they kept the faith.

February 8, 1999

Concluding Argument to the Senate

M r. Chief Justice, learned counsel, and the Senate, we are
blessedly coming to the end of this melancholy procedure, but before we gather up our papers and return to
the obscurity from whence we came, please permit me a few final
remarks.

First of all, I want to thank the Chief Justice not only for his
patience and his perseverance but for the aura of dignity that he has
lent to these proceedings, and it has been a great thrill really to be

This speech is cited in Joel J. Seidemann's *In the Interest of Justice: Great
Opening and Closing Arguments of the Last 100 Years (Regan Books, 2004).*

here in his company as well as in the company of you distinguished senators.

Secondly, I want to compliment the President's counsel. They have conducted themselves in the most professional way. They have made the most of a poor case, in my opinion.

Excuse me. There's an old Italian saying, that has nothing to do with the lawyers, but to your case, and it says: "You may dress the shepherd in silk, but he will still smell of the goat." But all of you are great lawyers and it's been an adventure being with you.

You know, the legal profession, like politics, is ridiculed pretty much, and every lawyer feels that and understands the importance of the rule of law—to establish justice, to maintain the rights of mankind, to defend the helpless and the oppressed, to protect innocence, to punish guilt. These are duties which challenge the best powers of man's intellect and the noblest qualities of the human heart. We are here to defend that bulwark of our liberty, the rule of law. As for the House managers, I want to tell you and our extraordinary staff how proud I am of your service. For myself, I cannot find the words to adequately express how I feel. I must use the inaudible language of the heart. I've gone through it all by your side, the media condemnations, the patronizing editorials, the hate mail, the insults hurled in public, the attempts at intimidation, the death threats, and even the disapproval of our colleagues, which cuts the worst.

You know, all a congressman ever gets to take with him when he leaves this building is the esteem of his colleagues and his constituents. We've risked that for a principle and for our duty as we've seen it.

In speaking to my managers of whom I am terminally proud, I can borrow the words of Shakespeare's "Henry V" as he addressed his little army of longbowmen at the battle of Agincourt, and he said: "We few—we happy few, we band of brothers. For he who sheds his blood with me shall be my brother. And gentlemen in England now abed will curse the fact that they are not here and hold their manhood cheap when any speaks who fought with us on St. Crispin's Day."

As for the juror judges, you distinguished Senators, it's always a victory for democracy when its elected representatives do their duty no matter how difficult and unpleasant, and we thank you for it.

Please don't misconstrue our fervor for our cause to any lack of respect or appreciation for your high office. But our most formidable opponent has not been opposing counsel nor any political party. It's been cynicism—the widespread conviction that all politics and all politicians are by definition corrupt and venal. That cynicism is an acid eating away at the vital organs of American public life. It is a clear and present danger because it blinds us to the nobility and the fragility of being a self-governing people.

One of the several questions that needs answer is whether your vote on conviction lessens or enlarges that cynicism. Nothing begets cynicism like the double standard—one rule for the popular and the powerful and another for the rest of us.

One of the most interesting things in this trial was the testimony of the President's good friend, the former Senator from Arkansas. He did his persuasive best to maintain the confusion that this is all about sex.

Of course it's useful for the defense to misdirect our focus toward what everyone concedes are private acts and none of our business, but if you care to read the articles of impeachment, you won't find any complaints about private, sexual misconduct. You will find charges of perjury and obstruction of justice which are public acts and federal crimes, especially when committed by the one person duty-bound to faithfully execute the laws.

Infidelity is private and non-criminal. Perjury and obstruction are public and criminal. The deliberate focus on what is not an issue here is the defense lawyer's tactic and nothing more. This entire saga has been a theater of distraction and misdirection. Time-honored defense tactics when the law and facts get in the way.

One phrase you have not heard the defense pronounce is the "sanctity of the oath," but this case deeply involves the efficacy, the meaning and the enforceability of the oath. The President's defenders stay away from the word "lie" preferring "mislead" or "deceived," but they shrink from the phrase "sanctity of the oath," fearing it as one might a rattlesnake.

There is a visibility factor in the president's public acts, and those which betray a trust or reveal contempt for the law are hard to sweep under the rug, or under the bed for that matter.

They reverberate, they ricochet all over the land and provide the worst possible example for our young people. As that third grader from Chicago wrote to me: "If you can't believe the President, who can you believe?"

Speaking of young people, in 1946 a British playwright, Terence Rattigan wrote a play based on a true experience that happened in England in 1910. The play was called 'The Winslow Boy.' And the story, a true story, involved a young 13-year-old lad who was kicked out of the Royal Naval College for having forged somebody else's signature on a postal money order.

Of course, he claimed he was innocent, but he was summarily dismissed and his family of very modest means couldn't afford legal counsel, and it was a very desperate situation. Sir Edward Carson, the best lawyer of his time—barrister I suppose—got interested in the case and took it on pro bono, and lost all the way through the courts.

Finally, he had no other place to go, but he dug up an ancient remedy in England called "petition of right." You ask the king for relief. And so Carson wrote out five pages of reasons why a petition of right should be granted. And lo and behold, it got past the attorney general and got to the king. The king read it, agreed with it, and wrote across the front of the petition: "Let right be done—Edward VII."

And I have always been moved by that phrase. I saw the movie, I saw the play, and I have the book, and I am still moved by that phrase "Let right be done." I hope when you finally vote that will move you, too.

There are some interesting parallels to our cause here today. This Senate chamber is our version of the House of Lords, and while we managers cannot claim to represent that 13-year-old Winslow boy, we speak for a lot of young people who look to us to set an example.

Ms. Seligman last Saturday said we want to win too badly. This surprised me, because none of the managers has committed perjury, nor obstructed justice, nor claimed false privileges. None has hidden evidence under anyone's bed, nor encouraged false testimony before the grand jury. That's what you do if you want to win too badly.

I believe it was Saul Bellow who once said, "A great deal of intelligence can be invested in ignorance when the need for illusion is great." And those words characterize the defense in this case— the need for illusion is great.

I doubt there are many people on the planet who doubt the President has repeatedly lied under oath and has obstructed justice. The defense spent a lot of time picking lint. There is a saying in equity, I believe, that equity will not stoop to pick up pins. But that was their case. So the real issue doesn't concern the facts, the stubborn facts, as the defense is fond of saying, but what to do about them.

I am still dumbfounded about the drafts of the censures that are circulating. We aren't half as tough on the President in our impeachment articles as this draft is that was printed in the *New York Times*. "An inappropriate relationship with a subordinate employee in the White House which was shameless, reckless and indefensible."

I have a problem with that. It seems they're talking about private acts of consensual sexual misconduct, which are really none of our business. But that's the lead-off.

Then they say the President "deliberately misled and deceived the American people and officials in all branches of the United States government." This is not a Republican document. This is coming from here.

"The President gave false or misleading testimony and impeded discovery of evidence in judicial proceedings." Isn't that another way of saying obstruction of justice and perjury? "The President's conduct demeans the office of the President as well as the President himself and creates disrespect for the laws of the land."

Future generations of Americans must know that such behavior is not only unacceptable, but bears grave consequences, including loss of integrity, trust, and respect—but not loss of job.

"Whereas William Jefferson Clinton's conduct has brought shame and dishonor to himself and to the office of the President; whereas he has violated the trust of the American people (see Hamilton *Federalist* Number 65), and he should be condemned in the strongest terms." Well, the next-to-the-strongest terms—the strongest terms would remove him from office.

Well, do you really cleanse the office as provided in the Constitution? Or do you use the air-wick of a censure resolution? Because any censure resolution, to be meaningful, has to punish the President—if only his reputation. And how do you deal with the laws of bill of attainder? How do you deal with the separation of powers? What kind of a precedent are you setting?

We all claim to revere the Constitution, but a censure is something that is advice, a way of avoiding the harsh Constitutional option, and it's the only one you have, either up or down on impeachment.

That, of course, is your judgment, and I am offering my views for what they're worth. Once in a while I do worry about the future. I wonder if after this culture war is over that we're engaged in, if an America will survive that's worth fighting to defend. People won't risk their lives for the UN or over the Dow Jones averages, but I wonder in future generations whether there'll be enough vitality left in duty, honor, and country to excite our children and grandchildren to defend America.

There's no denying the fact that what you decide will have a profound effect on our culture as well as on our politics. A failure to convict will make a statement that lying under oath, while unpleasant and to be avoided, is not all that serious. Perhaps we can explain this to those currently in prison for perjury.

We have reduced lying under oath to a breach of etiquette, but only if you are the President. Wherever and whenever you avert your eyes from a wrong, from an injustice, you become a part of the problem. On the subject of civil rights, it's my belief this issue doesn't belong to anyone. It belongs to everyone. It certainly belongs to those who have suffered invidious discrimination and one would have to be catatonic not to know that the struggle to keep alive equal protection of the law never ends.

The mortal enemy of equal justice is the double standard and if we permit a double standard, even for the President, we do no favor to the cause of human rights. It's been said that America has nothing to fear from this President on the subject of civil rights.

I doubt Paula Jones would subscribe to that endorsement. If you agree that perjury and obstruction of justice have been committed, and yet you vote down the conviction, you're expending and expanding the boundaries of permissible presidential conduct. You're saying a perjurer and an obstructor of justice can be president in the face of no less than three precedents for conviction of federal judges for perjury. You shred those precedents and you raise the most serious questions of whether the President is in fact subject to the law, or whether we are beginning a restoration of the divine rights of kings.

The issues we're concerned with have consequences far into the future, because the real damage is not to the individuals involved, but to the American system of justice and especially the principle that no one is above the law.

Edward Gibbon wrote his magisterial "Decline and Fall of the Roman Empire" in the late 18th century. In fact, the first volume was published in 1776. In his work, he discusses an emperor named Septimus Severus who died in 211 A.D. after ruling 18 years. And here's what Gibbon wrote about the emperor: "Severus promised only to betray; he flattered only to ruin; and however he might occasionally bind himself by oaths and treaties, his conscience, obsequious to his interest, always released him from the inconvenient obligation."

I guess those who believe history repeats itself are really onto something.

Horace Mann said: "You should be ashamed to die unless you have achieved some victory for humanity." To the House managers, I say your devotion to duty and the Constitution has set an example that is a victory for humanity. Charles de Gaulle once said France would not be true to herself if she wasn't engaged in some great enterprise. That's true of us all. We spend our short lives as consumers, space occupiers, clock watchers, spectators—or in the service of some great enterprise.

I believe being a Senator, being a Congressman, and struggling with all our might for equal justice for all is a great enterprise. It's our great enterprise. And to my House managers, your great enterprise was not to speak truth to power, but to shout it.

And now let us all take our place in history on the side of honor, and oh yes, let right be done.

Crises,
Conflicts,
and
Common
Sense

*Chairmen and ranking members of the House and Senate
International Relations and Armed Services Committees
meet with President George W. Bush; HJH sits to his right*

S omeone once said of Mississippi that the past isn't forgotten; in fact, the past isn't even past. That's true of more than the Magnolia State. It applies to world affairs in general. Let me illustrate. In the spring of 1989, an old woman by the name of Zita died at the age of 97. President Reagan had left office only two months earlier; his partner and successor, George Bush, was about to deal with the collapse of the Soviet Union. Everyone knew dramatic change was coming, though few suspected the suddenness with which it would appear. Then the Hungarian government opened its border with Austria, allowing free movement from eastern Europe to the West, and the remnants of the Iron Curtain elsewhere became obsolete. It was all over: the cruel division of peoples, the enslavement from the Baltic to the Mediterranean, the homicidal absurdity of Leninism—all of it was headed for the same trash heap as National Socialism and the other lunacies of the Twentieth Century. Zita, princess of Bourbon-Parma, last Empress of Austria and Queen of Hungary, had lived to see the end.

That was fitting, for Zita and her husband, the Emperor Karl, were the only rulers of their time who understood that the Great War of 1914 might destroy the civilization that had generated it. They alone tried to implement Pope Benedict XV's pleas for peace. They alone forbade the use of poison gas by their military. And in the end, they and their world were swept away by what, at the time, seemed like progress.

It has taken the better part of a century to get over the consequences of that progress. Indeed, the past is always with us, perhaps out of our sight and out of the world's memory just as was the exiled Empress Zita; but it is there, waiting to remind us that no one escapes from history. I tried to keep that in mind during my 6-year tenure as Chairman of the House Committee on International Relations (formerly, and now again, the Foreign Affairs Committee). In that capacity, I often was called upon to comment about world affairs. The speeches in this section reflect that special responsibility, though my interest in foreign policy goes much farther back than my chairmanship. Indeed, that interest has largely shaped my life.

There are fewer and fewer of us WWII vets around, so please permit me this one extended reminiscence. I was only 17 when Imperial Japan struck Pearl Harbor; but from that day on, the world outside the United States dominated my life. As a freshman at Georgetown University, the beneficiary of a basketball scholarship and waiting on tables for my tuition, I was part of the generation that never expected to be in places like New Guinea or Lingayen Gulf in the Philippines; but there I was, despite my youth, in charge of a Landing Craft Tank (LCT 1148) moving cargo and personnel around the Pacific. The kamikaze threat was bad enough, but my crew's gravest danger came when we were ordered out to the South China Sea to lighten a Liberty Ship, run aground on the rocks off the west coast of Luzon, before a typhoon hit. Bad timing: both the sky and sea turned an ugly shade of green, the waves were mountainous, and we had no navigational equipment. While our ship tossed about like a match box, I tried to reassure my crew even though I expected to drown any minute. Somehow we made it through the night and, by dawn's early light, saw the safety of Subic Bay way off in the distance.

In such places and in such circumstances millions of young Americans found themselves—and found as well a broader view of our country's role in the world. After all that we had experienced, it would never occur to us that there might be, as some young intellectuals more recently declared, an end to history.

I will never forget how my returning shipmates and I, knowing we would disembark at San Francisco in the morning, stayed up all night to catch the first sight of home: the dim amber lights of the Golden Gate Bridge. We were returning to an America newly aware of its interdependence with the rest of mankind. Gone forever was the isolationism symbolized in the 1920s by the legendary Bible-belt legislator who opposed teaching foreign languages in the public schools because, if English was good enough for Jesus Christ, it was good enough for the rest of us. Even so, during my pre-congressional years as a student (Georgetown, B.S.; Loyola University of Chicago, J.D., courtesy of the G.I. Bill—Thanks, Uncle Sam), a lawyer, and then a state legislator in Springfield, there was little chance to be involved in foreign policy. With my first election to Congress in 1974, however, I at last had the opportunity, even though almost eight years passed before I gained an appointment to the Foreign Affairs Committee.

Through it all, from my military service to my Chairmanship, I have had a constant philosophy. I am an internationalist, not in the sense that our country's interests do not come first, but in the sense that those interests are served best when America is fully engaged with the world, leading it by example, and prepared to decisively counter those who do not wish us well.

There are those who like to say that all politics is local. Nonsense. As someone who cut his political teeth in Chicago politics, I certainly understand ward and neighborhood politics, community dynamics, and regional needs and responsibilities. But the most important kind of politics transcends provincialism. It looks to the national good, and it seeks to understand the world. A few years back, a nationally prominent Member of the House—whose name I could share with you only by breaking a confidence, so I won't—while visiting a major Communist capital, had to be informed whose enormous portrait was draped across the Marxist government's building. It was Karl Marx himself, all bushy beard and glaring eyes. The irony should be instructive. Before Representatives or Senators, no matter now domestically powerful, presume to act on the world stage, especially as critics of their own government's policies, they would do well to better educate themselves about the human experience of the last two centuries or so. Perhaps they would then have a better appreciation for the role our country has undertaken in world affairs.

The conduct of foreign affairs is like a roller coaster ride, except the track keeps changing and one never knows where the car will eventually wind up. Consider the difference between foreign policy and its domestic counterpart, for example, tax policy or housing policy or welfare policy. In those latter cases, there are few surprises. The overall economy may slump, or fiscal restraints may tighten, but we are not going to be suddenly confronted by dramatically altered circumstances or radically different outlooks. That is why we can spend years, indeed decades, debating over and over the same points, whether it's the supply-side approach to the IRS code or federal vs. state responsibility for public assistance. Whatever movement we encounter in those debates, it is nothing compared to the abrupt, often wrenching changes that are the week to week fare in international relations.

The most obvious reason is that, in world affairs, anyone who gets a hand on power anywhere in the world is automatically a player in a very dangerous game. There is an almost unlimited number of unpredictable factors. Afghan warlords, freelance terrorists, a Venezuelan caudillo, African tribal armies—all these and many others of the same ilk demand the same level of attention as, say, the Prime Minister of the United Kingdom or the Secretary General of the U.N. In domestic policy, one can at least hope that a given problem will be "solved," as when the Congress created a range of nutrition programs to deal with hunger in America. In foreign policy, more often than not, problems are supplanted or overshadowed or become crises; they seem never to go away.

Two lessons I have learned from my three decades of congressional second-guessing about international affairs. The first is that there is no discontinuity in history. The more we try to understand a particular problem, the deeper we must delve into its past. The roots of the current imbroglio over Kosovo, for example, are much older than the American Republic, dating to the tragic battle there in 1389. The dreadful toll of Shiite-Sunni strife in Iraq stems from a succession dispute in 661. Today's conflict between Christians and Moslems across the southern rim of the Sahara continues an Islamic expansion in West Africa that got into high gear with the conversion of the kings of Ghana around the end of the first millennium. No wonder that, for contemporary Americans, whose idea of antiquity is the Watergate affair, the world remains a mystifying place.

My second lesson is that there is no inevitability in history. History, after all, is not forces or trends or currents; it is individuals choosing to act or not to act, and each of them responsible for his or her own choices. There was nothing inevitable about the success of the American Revolution; in fact, all the smart money should have been on the Brits. Absent Lincoln in the presidency, there was nothing inevitable about the continued existence of the United States, especially if James Buchanan had had another year or two in the White House. The fall of the European dynasties in WWI, the rise of Hitler, America's triumph in the Cold War—in each case, there could have been quite a different outcome. In each case, what made the difference was the vision and determination, or the lack thereof, among world leaders and those whom they inspire. That is what makes the difference today—and what will determine international events tomorrow.

Foreign policy, then, has to be a balancing act between those two lessons—no discontinuity and no inevitability—even when they seem to contradict one another. The genius of a successful foreign policy is to find ways for historical continuity to cut new channels, rather like a river that breaks through its horseshoe bend to start a new course, leaving the detritus of the past behind in the mud flats. President Reagan's dramatically different approach to the Soviet Union—a massive military build-up while offering our adversary the protection of a shared SDI, challenging the Soviet leader by name to tear down walls while publicly envisioning a Europe united from the Atlantic to the Urals—was a case in point. Reagan was fully aware of the way the tragic past had stacked the deck against his goals, but he was equally certain that fundamental things could fundamentally change.

With that in mind, I try to look ahead but know better than to make predictions. It is not likely that, in whatever is left of my own lifetime, we will be able to answer the three most important questions in international affairs. First, will China make the transition, not just to capitalism, but to a truly free and open society; or does its ongoing military buildup portend future confrontations with the United States, over Taiwan or other matters, as dangerous as the

Cuban Missile Crisis of 1962? Second, will Russia be integrated into western civilization before the vastness of central Asia and Siberia is overwhelmed by Islamic culture and Chinese demography? Third, can democracies rooted in the Judeo-Christian tradition survive the resurgence of Islam, or are we doomed for generations to reenact, in various venues and with modern firepower, the battle of Lepanto? There, in 1571, the Moslem assault against Christian Europe was forever halted, or so the West liked to believe for more than four hundred years, though those four centuries may have been only a lull in a much longer struggle. Perhaps our grandchildren may be able to answer those questions, though it is more likely that they will prefer to formulate their own.

Let me return to an idea already expressed herein—the role of individuals, rather than movements or forces, in determining the course of history—because that idea underlies most of what I have to say in the addresses that follow. The rebirth of post-war Europe, for example, would have been unlikely without the cooperation between the Democratic President Harry Truman, the Republican Senate Leader Arthur Vandenberg, and General George C. Marshall, Secretary of State, whose eponymous Plan to lift the Old World from economic ruin thwarted Stalin's greatest ambitions. Today's European Union, for a different example, rests on another triad: De Gaulle, Adenauer, and De Gaspari, three visionaries united by their common religious faith and belief in democracy, who bound together the three great nations of western Europe only a few years after the end of their fratricidal war. Their counterparts in eastern Europe, as living symbols of resistance to tyranny, were a quartet of cardinals: Wyszynski in Poland, Tomasek in Czechoslovakia, Mindzenti in Hungary, Stepinac in Yugoslavia. The honor role goes on: Solzhenitsyn, of course, Sakharov, John Paul II, and Armando Valladares, whose poems proved stronger than Castro's prison bars.

But one need not be famous to make a difference, even in world affairs. Lech Walesa, who led the Solidarity movement to a free Poland, was just another metalworker—but with a will of steel. He was fortunate that, in the spring of 1987, when Solidarity was hurting financially and western elites could not envisage its success, a congressional staff member, with the same steely determination, convinced a bipartisan group of senators to appropriate one million dollars for the organization. Another million came later in the year, when the staffer got Congressman Jack Kemp to take the lead in adding the cash to the foreign operations appropriation bill. Against the wishes of the State Department, yet another million came the next year too. Meanwhile, the same ingenious activist had secured an amendment to the Defense Authorization bill that threatened to cut off all trade with Poland if the Gomulka regime dared to arrest Solidarity activists. One man, Michael Hammond by name, did all that for no reason but the cause of liberty and for no reward except a clear conscience.

My point is that speeches, including the ones that follow this introduction, rarely make history. Determined individuals do. And if any one of the following talks has inspired others to stand more strongly for their beliefs and to act more boldly upon their principles, then will I feel justified in the thought and the passion with which I have tried to endow them.

March 7, 2001

The Crisis to Come

W e are honored today to have before us our new Secretary of State, Colin Powell, for the first of what we hope will be many appearances before our Committee. Mr. Secretary, I know I speak for all Members in extending to you our congratulations on your appointment and our wishes for your success. All of us are very eager to hear from you, but before recognizing you, I would like to exercise my prerogative as Chairman to offer a few thoughts. I will then recognize the distinguished Ranking Democratic Member, Mr. Lantos, to offer some remarks of his own.

As a new century opens, the United States finds itself at a unique moment, not only in its own history, but in that of the world as well. We stand at the pinnacle of power: in virtually every area—military, economic, technological, cultural, political—we enjoy a primacy that is unprecedented and virtually unchallenged. Our potential at times seems unlimited, to some perhaps even permanent.

When I ponder the world and America's role in it, there is indeed much to be thankful for, many accomplishments to take pride in, and much that inspires hope. But as pleasant as these thoughts may be, I confess that I also see much that concerns me. The source of that concern is not the long list of problems we daily confront around the globe nor even the possibility of some larger challenge in the near future that we cannot handle. These possibilities, of course, must command the attention of anyone who seriously contemplates America's place in the world, but I am confident that our resources are sufficient to handle the likely obstacles and dangers.

The concern I speak of is of the longer-term, specifically how well we will use the enormous power we currently possess to secure the future for our country and the generations to come. The wealth of opportunities we currently possess are not permanent; the luxury of choice may be a passing one. To believe that we shall always be above the fray, untouched and untouchable by the forces of destruction still at work in this world, is a dangerous illusion. Our current summer may yet prove fleeting.

The principal problem, the one that concerns me the most, is that we have no long-term strategy, no practical plan for shaping the future.

Nearly a decade has passed since the collapse of the Soviet Union, and without question the world is a vastly better place because of it. But the fall of that empire took with it the central organizing principle of our foreign policy for the last half-century. Now I have read and heard many learned discourses and debates on what the new U.S. agenda should be, but I confess that I have yet to see a compelling path identified that shows us how we should use the power we currently possess to bring into being the world we want.

Instead of a firm course, I see drift. Instead of shaping the evolution of events in pursuit of long-term objectives, we have been busy responding to problems as they arise, guided by an agenda that has been more thrust upon us by circumstances than one we have ourselves constructed for our own purposes.

That is not to say that many remarkable things have not been accomplished in the past decade—the dismantling of the Soviet empire and the liberation of the eastern half of Europe; the expansion of NATO; the passage of the North American Free Trade Agreement; the continued spread of democracy; the resolute defense of our allies and the containment of our enemies around the world.

But these and other successes are no substitute for a long-term vision. Not only do we risk leaving the future to chance, we gamble with what we have come to take for granted. Let me illustrate my point with a couple of examples.

I believe we are watching the beginnings of an unraveling of the Atlantic relationship. By the Atlantic relationship, I mean something more than just NATO. I mean the entire complex of connections between North America and Europe, the close identity of interests, that we and our allies have constructed out of the ashes of World War II. This relationship is the very foundation of the postwar international system, the irreplaceable center on which the stability of the globe depends. It is from this core that the democratic and economic revolution now transforming the world has spread.

That relationship is fraying. Slowly, quietly, it is being hollowed out, even as the responsible officials solemnly reaffirm their commitment. There is no crisis to compel action, but I fear that should a crisis come, it will be too late.

Closer to home, there is Mexico. Our two countries have kept each other at arm's length for virtually our entire histories, and both countries are the poorer for it. But we cannot escape the fate that geography has decreed for us; there is no other country on the planet which has the potential to affect us so broadly, so immediately. We are in the process of transforming each other. Mexico is currently undergoing the most hopeful revolution in its long history, the success or failure of which will have a profound impact on the United States. They cannot be allowed to fail.

Now, the President is to be congratulated for his understanding and recognition of Mexico's importance, signified by his use of the term "a special relationship" to characterize our ties, a designation hitherto reserved only for our closest allies. But when I look more closely at how we actually intend to assist Mexico's entry into the ranks of the developed world, I have trouble identifying any guiding strategy on our part.

As for Asia, that giant continent veers between great hope and great chaos. China's rise to a world status commensurate with the immense resources of its people is a certainty. That rise, and the aspirations which must accompany it, cannot but impact the system we and our allies have brought forth and maintained in East Asia since World War II. Our hope is that democracy will, in time, tame this potential challenge, but there is no guarantee that we will win that race, and we may be faced with difficult decisions much more quickly than our planners have assumed. In Asia, one can point to many areas of progress, and many areas of concern, and I have no doubt that your attention will be sorely taxed by the current and future problems that region will unfailingly produce. But again I ask: what is our long-term strategy toward this region? How do our goals there fit into our global objectives?

A similar inquiry can be constructed for every region: the Middle East, South Asia, Latin America, Africa. And there are a long list of other concerns: terrorism, the many assaults on human rights, the stability of the international financial system, the trade in weapons and narcotics and on and on, as many as one would care to list. There are far more than enough to overwhelm our attention and to keep us and our successors busy indefinitely. So I say again: what concerns me most is that, in the crush of the present, there is little or no evidence of the development of a long-term strategy, no identification of a clear destination toward which we should be heading. Instead, for all of our undoubted power, we often seem to be at the mercy of the currents, carried downstream toward an uncertain destination instead of moving toward one of our own choosing. And while our attention is transfixed on the latest crisis that CNN has decided must be dealt with, the underlying structures are shifting, and historic opportunities fading.

Despite our power, we must resist the temptation of believing we can fix every problem, indulge in every wish. Part of our strategy must be to decide what we cannot do, what we choose not to do, and to ensure that others take up their responsibilities.

I raise this issue not because I have a ready solution to offer, but because I fear that no one else does, either. But a practical, long-term vision is sorely needed; it is a prerequisite that we dare not postpone until some more convenient time. I say this not as a Republican; indeed, there is no hope of success unless it is broadly bipartisan. We need consensus in this body and in this city, as well as the support of the American people.

So, even as we revel in our good fortune, my great hope is that we will use this gift of time to plan for the future, unhurried, uncoerced, but mindful of the task at hand, aware that our opportunity to do so is a mortal one. Our choice is clear: We can endeavor to shape the future or simply allow it to shape us.

A century ago, Britain stood majestically at the height of her power; within forty years, the knife was at her throat, and she survived only because the United States was there to rescue her. But, Mr. Secretary, as you are well aware, there is no one to rescue us. That is why we must think long and hard about how we can use the opportunities that Providence and the labors of two centuries have provided us to so shape the world that the need for rescue never occurs.

Despite this concern, I greet the future with soaring hope. I believe our new president and secretary of state bring qualities of leadership to this critical endeavor, and I have confidence that we will prevail.

July 13, 2001

Commonwealth of the Americas

T hank you for the opportunity to speak to the graduating class of the Western Hemisphere Institute for Security Cooperation.

This Institute has a broad and important mandate: to train soldiers, law enforcement officers, and civilians from the Western Hemisphere to enhance security in their countries and the region as a whole, while also strengthening democracy, deepening the rule of law, and safeguarding human rights. This mission is in keeping with the very real challenges we face in the 21st Century: peacekeeping, resolving border conflicts peacefully, responding to natural disasters, and—as ideological conflict has given way to new threats—combating the illicit drug trade and international criminal organizations.

Today, I would like to address the future of our hemisphere. This is fitting because you, as professional soldiers, law enforcement officials, and civilian leaders, have an important role to play in seeing that this vision becomes a reality.

The United States is a global power, with global interests and responsibilities. Given this open-ended outlook, it is not surprising that our attention is thinly spread and easily captured by the many pressing problems of the world. At times it seems that the United States has become the world's fire brigade, racing from one alarm to another, battling an unending series of conflagrations in far-off places, with most of the other countries watching it all from the sidelines. Whatever its merits, this ad hoc approach comes at a great cost: our agenda is shaped more by a scattered, reflexive response to the latest problems than by a conscious effort to shape events in pursuit of our long-term interests.

This certainly has been the case with Latin America, which has long been relegated to the periphery of U.S. foreign policy. Despite this inattention, it will come as a surprise to many that the United States has been presented with an opportunity of enormous consequence: to bring into being a permanent zone of peace, prosperity, and security throughout the entire Western Hemisphere, a self-sustaining equilibrium that could well become a model for the rest of the world. This initiative could rightly be termed the Commonwealth of the Americas.

This is not a utopian vision; much of the foundation for this Commonwealth has already been laid, the product of several decades of effort that extends to virtually every country in North and South America. Its most prominent achievements include the spread of democracy, the embrace of free markets, the defeat of communism and other threats to freedom, and a growing recognition that the interests of individual countries are best advanced through cooperation and an openness to the world. Despite their undoubted benefits, however, these accomplishments have no guarantee of permanence. In fact, many are under threat even as we speak. If they are to be made lasting, if their promise is to be fully realized, we must seize this historic opportunity to reshape our hemisphere and preserve its blessings indefinitely.

For the United States, establishing an overall objective of securing this hemispheric Commonwealth would allow us to weave together and give focus to our current assemblage of individual policies toward the region. But the United States is only one part of the necessary equation: the prerequisite for the Commonwealth is a recognition by all of the countries of the hemisphere that each shares a common interest in the well-being and security of the region and that each country must shoulder its share of the responsibility for sustaining these.

The idea of collective responsibility will sound new to some ears due to the old stereotype of a powerful U.S. imposing its will on the smaller states to its south. The truth, however, is that the U.S. now is as much acted upon as acting. Let me cite one example: the North American Free Trade Agreement (NAFTA). This historic agreement committed Mexico, the U.S., and Canada to the creation of a continental economy, one with far-reaching effects beyond the purely economic. I believe this agreement is very much in the long-term interests of the United States. However, and contrary to the popular imaginings, NAFTA was not a U.S. initiative, but a Mexican one, not a U.S. device to exploit Mexico but an embrace sought by Mexico to advance its entry into the modern world. It represents a long-delayed recognition that the interests of both Mexico and the U.S. are best advanced through cooperation and that the distance and hostility that have characterized our relations for two centuries have imposed great costs on both countries.

I cite the NAFTA both as a model for a broader cooperation and also to emphasize that every country has a role to play in setting the common agenda. That agenda may contain many things, but I believe that its core should center on promoting economic opportunity, security, and political freedom throughout the hemisphere.

Economic Opportunity

Our hopes for this hemisphere rest upon the economic advancement of all. Fortunately, our prospects are quite positive: during the 1990s, almost every country in our region embraced the free market and implemented a far-reaching series of economic reforms, thereby laying the foundation for sustained growth. We are only at the beginning of that process, however. Too many people in this rich hemisphere remain poor; too many are denied access to opportunities to better their lot and that of their families.

There are many obstacles that need to be overcome, and every country has an unfinished agenda. But one easy way to expand economic opportunity for every country in this hemisphere is to remove our antiquated and self-limiting barriers to trade. This is what the Free Trade Area of the Americas (FTAA) represents: the recognition that protectionism is a dead-end street and that the economic interests of each country are best advanced through cooperation and an openness to the world.

President Bush has rightly made the FTAA the centerpiece of U.S. policy towards the hemisphere, but it faces many hurdles, especially in the U.S. We are in the ironic situation that the greatest advocates of this agreement are the countries of Central and South America which formerly blockaded themselves against virtually every U.S. proposal for expanded cooperation. Now it is they who are knocking on our door, preaching the benefits of cooperation, only to be met by repeated delays and excuses on our part. I believe that, ultimately, good sense will prevail in the U.S. and the FTAA will have a belated birth, but it will not be an easy fight.

Security

The defeat of the Soviet Union freed the world from a malevolent force that was the enemy of freedom everywhere. Today, our hemisphere is confronted with other formidable threats. Chief among them is the drug trade because the criminal empire behind it has joined forces with armed insurgencies in a number of areas. In the Andes there is the unsettling prospect of democratically elected governments being overcome by challenges too great for its resources to handle. But an even more disturbing scenario is that of criminal organizations freeing themselves from the restraints of government altogether, becoming masters in their own territory and virtually sovereign actors in the world. Can any government, any person in our hemisphere not regard that prospect as frightening?

Many believe that the drug trade is the United States' problem because we are the principal consumers. But the belief that other countries can serve merely as transit routes, and perhaps even profit from doing so while remaining untouched, is a great error. Everywhere the drug trade produces massive corruption, cultivates violence, undermines the authority of governments, bankrolls insurgencies, and eventually turns its malevolent focus on the local population.

I cite the drug problem as one that requires cooperation throughout the region, but I could list many others as well. Given that cooperation, even a goal as ambitious as making war impossible in our hemisphere is within our grasp, beginning with the renunciation of all territorial claims by one state against any other. Similarly, preventing the intrusion of any outside power requires only a common determination on our part. But the content of any list is less important than the recognition that the establishment of a secure environment throughout the entire hemisphere is a responsibility shared by every country in the region. Once that is secured, everything else becomes possible.

Political Freedom

Political freedom, prosperity, and security are all related; each requires the others if it is to be fully realized and made secure.

The 1990s witnessed great strides forward for democracy in the hemisphere. But even as we celebrate this enormous progress, we recognize that it is threatened in many areas. Those threats come from many sources, both internal and external.

While we must respect the right of countries to determine their own course through democratic means, we cannot accept the overthrow of democracy or the suppression of human rights in any of them, however pressing the emergency. We have a collective responsibility to oppose the seizure of power in any country by anyone, especially by the unelected and the self-appointed, and also to ensure that human rights are fully respected in practice as well as on paper.

But political freedom consists of more than simply free elections, although these are its indispensable precondition; and liberty is more than a series of grand pronouncements. Political freedom cannot be a grant of government, to be limited or withdrawn altogether when those in power see fit to do so. To be secure, it must exist as a permanent right and rest upon institutions of civil society that are sufficiently robust to be able to withstand any adverse pressure from the government.

That brings me to the role of U.S. assistance. The U.S. does have a role to play in promoting prosperity, security, and political freedom throughout the hemisphere, one we share with every other country. But that aid must be formulated in the recognition that the responsibility for promoting these benefits lies with the individual countries and societies, and that all the aid in the world cannot substitute for their indifference. Given that understanding, any assistance we provide should be aimed at promoting the private sector and strengthening the institutions of civil society, without which there can be no stable democracy or economic progress.

Conclusion

Following Columbus' accidental discovery of our continents, the Old World of Europe was transformed by the wealth found here and further enriched by the dreams these new lands made possible. Among the greatest gifts this New World held was the promise of a new beginning, one unencumbered by the oppression, the rigid structures, the limitations of the Old. In this new land, the dead hand of the past could be thrown off and possibilities that appeared utopian in their homeland could here be made real.

In many ways, we have lived up to that hope, but much remains to be accomplished before this hemisphere's promise is fully realized. The first step in that process is to recognize that our fates are joined together. The second is a commitment to act together to make real the opportunity that lies before us: to bring into being the Commonwealth of the Americas and to make of our hemisphere a New World for all the ages to come.

August 24, 2001

China, Taiwan and Our Future

I would like to speak to you today about China, Taiwan, and the future of U.S. foreign policy toward the region. In the new century, the world will be reinvented once again, as it was in the one just past. We cannot yet have confidence that the outcome will favor us. The known and the comfortable may vanish; enemies may become friends and friends enemies; unseen dangers and unguessed opportunities lie in wait. Knowing this, we would be wise to step back from our focus on the present and consider what the future may bring, for we must be prepared for whatever may happen.

To do that, we must begin with an idea of what is to come. As always, consensus will be elusive. A hundred observers likely would produce a hundred different forecasts of the next few decades, from the bleak to the optimistic. Yet, amid this competition of viewpoints, there is one development on which unanimity reigns: China's certain emergence as a world power.

How quickly that emergence will take place and the path it will follow are subjects of great disagreement, even among the experts; but few doubt that the impact on the United States and the world will be profound, from the economic and technological to the cultural and political. It is my hope that its contribution will prove to be overwhelmingly positive, but neither individuals nor nations can operate in this world solely on hope. We must consider the possibility of less positive outcomes as well.

We cannot know for certain the course of China's emergence, but that does not excuse us from the need to prepare for several contingencies. For better or worse, the United States has become the principal guarantor of stability and order in the international system, a responsibility which we may revise but from which we cannot escape. Already there are many troubling signs that the regime in Beijing is moving toward policies that are not only inimical to stability in the international system but which are deliberately aimed at undermining U.S. interests around the world. This is no accident: if Beijing's ambition is to unilaterally revise the status quo in East Asia or elsewhere to its liking, it must first target the influence of the United States.

Once distant and abstract, the challenge posed by a powerful China was recently made tangible by Beijing's outrageous behavior regarding the U.S. surveillance plane forced down on the island of Hainan. The suddenness of the confrontation, and the unwarranted hostility toward the U.S. emanating from that country—along with, it must be said, Beijing's clear determination to humiliate us and its cynical encouragement of a xenophobic nationalism—offer a preview of the increasingly unpleasant possibilities that may lie in wait.

If a challenge is to come, it will be in East Asia, where the impact of China's emergence will first be felt. And it will center on Taiwan.

The regime in Beijing appears determined to bring about Taiwan's subordination, a determination so strong that, at times, it has even seemed willing to risk an armed confrontation. Its strategic planning and war gaming assume an increasingly prominent place for conflict with the U.S., especially in the Taiwan Straits. As China grows stronger and bolder, the potential for an actual clash seems only to increase.

For this and other reasons, there are those in the U.S. who regard our ties to Taiwan as a major liability, a relic of the Cold War which is not only dangerous but is an unnecessary obstacle to better relations between the U.S. and China. To some, the choice is not a difficult one: China is 50 times the size of Taiwan and good relations with Beijing are a self-evident necessity.

Not surprisingly, there are some in the U.S. who advocate that the U.S. and China should reach an accommodation over Taiwan. This line of argument has taken many forms over the past three decades, ever since President Nixon traveled to Beijing in 1972, but the recommendation is essentially the same: we should back off from Taiwan in return for improved relations with Beijing.

Although some have grown used to regarding Taiwan as a liability, this approach obscures Taiwan's true importance. For a free and uncoerced Taiwan is of immense strategic importance to the U.S. and to the world as a whole, perhaps an irreplaceable one. In fact, a free Taiwan is the key to the possibility of genuinely close relations between the U.S. and China and a guarantee that China's growing impact on the international system will be a positive one. It may even hold the key to China's destiny.

However, before I elaborate on this open-ended assertion, let me first set the context of U.S. policy toward China and the world.

As I noted at the beginning of my remarks, China's growing presence in the international system poses a number of possible dangers. A closer examination reveals that the challenge is only partly due to China's enormous size and economic dynamism. The real problem lies in the nature of the ruling regime.

The most worrisome specter facing the world is of a China grown powerful but still controlled by an authoritarian regime. By definition, non-democratic regimes have too few restraints on their freedom of action. The most extreme example was Mao's experimentation with ruinous economic and social policies that ultimately led to the starvation of millions and decades of chaos. When the regime's experiments were confined to China itself, the result was horrific domestically, but of little direct threat to the wider world. But a powerful China venturing out into the world will have the means to affect far more than just the lives of its own citizens.

There can be little doubt that the authoritarian regime now ruling in Beijing is a vast improvement over the Maoist dictatorship that preceded it. In the two decades since the Chinese leadership began to abandon its Marxist past and relax its stranglehold on the economy and on society, the Chinese people have used the narrow freedoms granted them to create an increasingly vibrant economy and freer, wealthier, and more secure lives for themselves.

Unfortunately, the economic liberalization that has so dramatically transformed China has not yet produced a corresponding political liberalization. Although the regime has allowed the Chinese people a greater zone of freedom in their personal and public lives, these freedoms are strictly limited and may be narrowed or withdrawn at the whim of the regime. Even these modest freedoms require a grateful docility from the population. Innocent efforts to organize outside of the Party's control are still repressed quite brutally. One need only recall the images of unarmed students being shot down in Tien an Men Square to know the regime's attitude toward attempts at actual democratization.

Many observers believe that the gradually expanding reforms have put China on an irreversible course toward a true market economy and toward increasing personal and political freedoms. In their eyes, liberalization is an inevitability. I very much hope this is the case.

But can anyone even remotely familiar with the history of the 20th Century claim to believe in the irreversibility of progress? Did not Hitler come to power in the most advanced country in Europe, preceded by several decades of liberalization throughout the continent? In the end, none of these were able to prevent Germany's return to a pagan past or to stop Hitler from making real his murderous fantasies.

However, were the ruling regime to extensively liberalize, perhaps even democratize, the challenges posed by China would greatly diminish. Allowed to determine their own affairs, the Chinese people, as is the case with all free peoples, likely would focus their efforts and attention on improving their lives and those of their families and countrymen rather than on foreign adventures. The prospect of conflict with the outside world would be greatly reduced and perhaps eliminated altogether.

A democratic China is a joyful prospect and would be the best possible outcome, both for the Chinese people and for the world. Can we do anything to improve its odds?

The limited instruments we possess—broadcasts of uncensored news, support for democracy groups, exposure of the regime's human rights abuses, and so forth—would appear to be grossly inadequate to the task. After all, China is a giant and ancient country, and democratization by remote control is unlikely to prove effective.

However, the U.S. can also bring to bear a unique strategic asset of immense value, but one that has lain too long dormant: our natural alliance with the peoples of the world.

All over the world, the populations in unfree countries look to the U.S., not because of our power or our material prosperity, but because of our ideals. Our country was founded on universal principles, ones we believe are applicable to every people. As Americans, we are inheritors of democracy and the rule of law, which evolved over centuries of bloody struggle with tyranny. Democracy assigns intrinsic value to human beings—to every member of the human family. Our Declaration of Independence, our country's birth certificate, explicitly states that the source of human dignity is our "Creator," and the right to life and liberty is "unalienable." Even as I speak, the power of these ideals continues to inspire legions of brave and often isolated individuals around the world to take on seemingly impossible odds.

That is true in China as well. When the courageous people in Tien an Men Square erected their Statue of Freedom, when they quoted from our founding documents, they were not looking to the U.S. for assistance in their unequal struggle. They did so in order to clearly demonstrate that the goals they sought for their country were shaped with the same ideals as those with which America has become identified and which are, indeed, a universal aspiration.

We rejoice when an unfree people secures their freedom, but we should understand that this represents more than merely a confirmation of our ideals. Simply put, freedom for others advances America's strategic interests. The advancement of those interests comes not by imposing our agenda on others but by helping the oppressed liberate themselves.

The Soviet Union provides the clearest example. For nearly half a century, by means of an enormous investment of labor and treasure, we succeeded in blocking Soviet expansion, while our economic and technological advances pressured the regime into competing at an increasing disadvantage. But what ultimately destroyed that empire was the determination of its subject peoples to liberate themselves. In securing their freedom, they fatally undermined the Soviet Union and in so doing gave the free world an incalculable strategic victory.

The example of the Soviet Union provides us with many profound lessons. Perhaps the most important is the power of words and symbols to inspire millions to a common cause.

To defy the Soviet regime was to take on seemingly impossible odds. To secure its rule, the regime trained its vast powers on all who would dissent, dividing and isolating the population in an effort to deny hope to any challengers. But the West was able to provide hope anyway, with the role of two individuals being especially critical. The first was the election of Pope John Paul II. His initial message to his countrymen in Poland told them: "Be not afraid." From that beginning, a mass movement took shape, Solidarity was born, and the Polish regime began its unstoppable slide to oblivion. Poland is now free.

Equally significant was the election of Ronald Reagan. Against the advice of many, Reagan refused to tame his remarks about the Soviet Union. When he called the Soviet Union "an evil empire," he was openly derided by many in the West as an ideologue or a warmonger. But veterans of the democracy movement in the former Soviet Union point to that statement as a turning point in their struggle. For it was the first time that a Western leader had called the Soviet Union by its real name, had openly stated that the regime was illegitimate and proclaimed it mortal. It was an unambiguous statement that, at long last, America was casting its lot with the people and not with the regime, a declaration that we would never abandon the oppressed merely to secure better relations with their oppressors.

That infusion of hope, the unambiguous declaration that America was openly aligning itself with those who were struggling against impossible odds, was a major element in setting in motion the events which dissolved the Soviet Union, almost without a shot being fired. Decades of pressure by the West on the Soviet Union was essential to its demise, but it was the victory of our allies within—the unfree peoples of the Soviet Union—which actually vanquished the empire.

In China, the regime is employing a new version of the old Soviet strategy toward advocates of political liberalization, including an attempt to isolate the population from the outside world and prevent free communication and organization. Essential to its continued tenure in power is the elimination of any hope that a change of regime is possible.

That is where the U.S. can play an essential role. The knowledge that the United States supports their efforts, that it is choosing them over the regime, would be of immense importance to members of the beleaguered Chinese democracy movement. The regime will not allow them to speak, but the regime cannot silence us.

How can we best do this? By publicly proclaiming that it is and will remain the goal of the United States to help the people of China peacefully bring to power a democratic government that they have chosen in free and fair elections. Our President should make this statement openly, and the Congress should do so as well. We should repeat it at every opportunity until the people of China and the regime know that it is an enduring objective.

This does not mean that we should break our ties with the regime. To the contrary, these should proceed as normal and even be enhanced. We should not threaten any intervention, nor impose any sanctions. Our economic ties, which are essential to China's modernization, should continue and even deepen. The regime will have no legitimate basis for complaint. But even as we continue our necessary relations with it, we should feel free to talk past the regime and directly to the people.

Our goal should be to convince the Chinese people that their victory is inevitable, to give them hope that the current regime and its vast powers of coercion are destined to fade. When they become confident of that future, the regime will have lost its power to make the population helpless by denying them hope. And once again, their victory will be freedom's victory, hopefully without a shot ever being fired.

So what is Taiwan's role in all of this? It is, quite simply, the key to this future. The regime in Beijing attempts to hold on to power by combining repression with the claim that only its unchallenged rule can guarantee continued peace and development. It says that democracy in China is impossible, and that any attempt to establish it would bring only a return to the upheaval and chaos of the past.

But this is a lie, and Taiwan is the proof of it. For decades, experts in the West and in China itself said that democracy was alien to Chinese culture, that it could never be applied successfully. But all of this was disproven in 1996, when for the first time in China's five millennia of recorded history, a democratically elected government took office. Given its potential meaning, this was an epochal event, one of the great triumphs of the century, but one that I regret was too little recognized around the world.

This historic accomplishment was further enhanced last year when a ruling party peacefully gave up power after losing at the polls. Elections are rare enough in this world, but peaceful transfers of power are rarer still and are the indisputable mark of the establishment of a genuine democracy and political freedom. With this transfer of power, Taiwan demonstrated that at last it had become a true democracy. And let me emphasize that it is a Chinese democracy.

And what happened? The sky has not fallen; progress did not give way to chaos. Instead, as political freedom and democracy grew stronger, so did Taiwan. For the reality is that political freedom and progress are not only compatible; together they thrive.

The advent of democracy does not mean that change has ceased; it is only beginning. Democracy brings with it a dynamism which some mistakenly see as instability. I know that the political situation in Taiwan lately has been undergoing significant changes. Political realignments are taking place; old and familiar structures are disappearing and new and untested ones are taking their place.

Many might view this as a cause for concern, but it is actually a sign of strength, an indication that change and adaptation are possible, that the political system is responding to the ever-changing demands of society. In America, political dynamism is a fact of life, and a welcome one, for it means that our system is working.

What does Taiwan's success mean for China? Taiwan's economic success was essential in convincing Beijing that a Western, market-oriented economic model would work in China. Now it is time for Taiwan's democratic model to have the same effect, only this time the audience is the Chinese population.

Taiwan's mere existence as a prosperous and stable Chinese democracy is a challenge to the regime in Beijing because it is proof that its propaganda about the impossibility of democracy in China is false. Democracy is not only possible in China; it already exists. Taiwan proves that an authoritarian regime is not necessary for stability and for progress, that democracy will actually enhance these. This great truth is not limited to Taiwan; it embraces all of China.

This is a deeply disquieting message to the regime, even if delivered quietly. I believe it is one reason why the regime in Beijing is so determined to bring Taiwan under its control.

So that there is no ambiguity, no misunderstanding, the United States must publicly state that we will never allow Beijing to subvert or destroy the world's only functioning Chinese democracy and thereby eliminate its subtle, yet powerful influence on the Chinese people. The eventual freedom of 1/5 of humanity is simply too important to us and to the future of the world.

Instead of backing away from Taiwan, we should hold its democracy up as an inspiring example to all of China. We must protect it, not only because we have a duty to come to the defense of freedom, but because it provides tangible hope that the world's largest nation, with its ancient and profound civilization, will one day enter the ranks of the free nations of the world.

Again let me stress our hope and expectation that the advent of democracy in China will be a peaceful one. We do not seek conflict. China is not now our enemy, nor need she ever be. Only tragedy could come from such a foolish mistake. To avoid that fate, our efforts to encourage democracy must include helping China become fully integrated into the world, from enhanced trade and personal exchanges to the Internet and the rule of law. The closer and more unconstrained the connections between China and the outside world, the more certain the advance of freedom.

That includes increasing economic links and dialog across the Taiwan Strait. These are of great importance to all concerned, and we hope that they will contribute to a lessening of tensions and to a peaceful resolution of the many issues involved.

In the end, China's fate is in the hands of her long-suffering people. Their freedom must be won largely through their own efforts, but America does have an important role to play in this momentous struggle. Our help can take many forms, but in the end, nothing will be of greater importance than our resolute commitment to democracy and freedom in China through the trials that lie ahead and our pledge to the Chinese people that we shall remain with them until they are free, however long the struggle.

In the depths of America's civil war, our greatest president, Abraham Lincoln, characterized the conflict as being not just for the present but for the "vast future also." That vast future is what I speak of here today. For by helping the Chinese people achieve their long-delayed freedom, we will ensure our own, and that of all the generations to come.

Thank you for allowing me to speak with you today.

June 17, 2002

Speaking to Our Silent Allies

As Americans, we are justly proud of our country. If any nation has been a greater force for good in the long and tormented history of this world, I am unaware of it. We have guarded whole continents from conquest, showered aid on distant lands, sent thousands of youthful idealists to remote and often inhospitable areas to help the world's forgotten.

Why, then, when we read or listen to descriptions of America in the foreign press, do we so often seem to be entering a fantasyland of hatred? Much of the popular press overseas, often including the government-owned media, daily depict the United States as a force for evil, accusing this country of an endless number of malevolent plots against the world. Even as we strike against the network of terrorists who masterminded the murder of thousands of Americans, our actions are widely depicted in the Muslim world as a war against Islam. Our efforts, however imperfect, to bring peace to the Middle East spark riots that threaten governments that dare to cooperate with us.

How has this state of affairs come about? How is it that the country that invented Hollywood and Madison Avenue has allowed such a destructive and parodied image of itself to become the intellectual coin of the realm overseas? Over the years, the images of mindless hatred directed at us have become familiar fixtures on our television screens.

All this time, we have heard calls that "something must be done." But, clearly, whatever has been done has not been enough.

I believe that the problem is too great and too entrenched to be solved by tweaking an agency here or reshuffling a program there. If a strategy is not working, we should not insist on more of the same. Instead, we must begin by rethinking our entire approach.

It is increasingly clear that much of the problem lies in our ineffective and often antiquated methods. For example, broadcasts on short-wave radio simply cannot compete with AM and FM channels in terms of accessibility, to say nothing of television, the most powerful medium of all. Shifting our efforts into these and other broad-based media, including the Internet and others, will take time and money, but this reorientation is a prerequisite to reaching our intended audience.

But there is a deeper problem. According to many observers, we have largely refused to participate in the contest for public opinion and thereby allowed our enemies' slanders to go unchallenged. The effort to avoid controversy has come at the cost of potential persuasion and of much of the reason to listen to us at all.

The results are sobering. In testimony last year before the House International Relations Committee, the Chairman of the Broadcasting Board of Governors, which oversees our international broadcasting efforts, stated that "we have virtually no youthful audience under the age of 25 in the Arab world."

We have several tasks, then. We must develop both the means of reaching a broader audience and also the compelling content that will persuade them to tune in. These objectives will not be easy to accomplish, especially in an increasingly competitive media environment, but they are prerequisite to our having an opportunity to present our case in clear and persuasive terms. Our work does not stop there, for we must make our case not once but over and over again and be prepared to do so for decades to come.

It is for that reason that I have introduced legislation aimed at accomplishing these and other goals, legislation which I am proud to say enjoys broad bipartisan support. This bill, H.R. 3969, is divided into three sections. The first reshapes and refocuses the State Department's public diplomacy programs, including specifying a series of objectives to be attained and requiring an annual plan be formulated to determine how these are to be implemented. Far greater prominence will be given to public diplomacy throughout all of the Department's activities, and greater resources will be made available to ensure that these new responsibilities can be met.

The second section establishes a series of exchange programs focused on the Muslim world. Our purpose here is to lay the foundation for long-term change in a part of the world to which we have given far too little attention. As we respond to the immediate problems before us, we must remember that the task we face has no obvious endpoint.

The third section of the bill reorganizes our international broadcasting services in order to prepare them for far-reaching and innovative reforms. Given the importance of broadcasting to our larger purpose, we cannot afford to be constrained by how we have always done things. New approaches and enhanced resources will be central to any prospect of winning an expanded audience, and this bill is but the first step in that direction. To this end, we have authorized $135 million to launch an ambitious effort into television broadcasting.

This bill has already passed our committee unanimously, and the House will soon have an opportunity to take it up. Then we will move on to the Senate with the intention of giving the President a bill to sign later this year.

Permit me to speak now of the larger purpose of our public diplomacy efforts. To some, that purpose is self-evident: to provide objective news and information, to convey an accurate and positive image of America, and to present and explain U.S. foreign policy.

Unquestionably, these are essential functions. If we do them well, they will comprise an indispensable voice of clarity regarding our foreign policy, one otherwise absent from the world's airways.

However, I believe that public diplomacy's potential is even greater. To understand that, we must first understand that half of our foreign policy is missing.

Let me explain.

As the most powerful actor in the international system, the U.S. conducts the world's only global foreign policy, one that dwarfs in extent and resources that of any other country. Its range extends across the entire spectrum, from the political and military to the economic and cultural, and centers on an elaborate array of relationships with virtually every sovereign government, from Russia to Vatican City, with scores of international organizations rounding out the total.

Nevertheless, for some years now, scholars have talked about the emergence in world politics of what they call "non-state actors." While the nation-state remains the primary "actor" on the world stage, it is no longer the only one—and in certain instances, what nation-states do and don't do is heavily conditioned by what those non-state actors do and don't do.

Poland's Solidarity movement in the 1980's is a powerful example of a "non-state actor" which had a dramatic and positive impact on the course of events. I needn't remind you that Al Qaeda has demonstrated a contrary ability to sow destruction.

Thus, it should be obvious to all that the dynamics of world politics are no longer determined by foreign policy professionals only. As important as they are, what they think and do is conditioned by what is happening in the hearts and minds of almost 7 billion human beings on a shrinking globe in an age of almost instantaneous information. That is why public diplomacy—the effort to persuade those hearts and minds of the truth about our purposes in the world—must be a crucial part of our foreign policy effort.

My point is this: Our focus on our relations with foreign governments and international organizations has led us to overlook a set of powerful allies: the peoples of the world.

Uniquely among the world's powers, a dense network connects the United States with the populations of virtually every country on the planet, a network that is independent of any formal state-to-state interaction. On one level, this is not surprising: as the preeminent political, military, and economic power, the presence of the United States is a daily fact of life in most areas of the globe. America's cultural impact is even broader, penetrating to the most forbiddingly remote areas of the world, with a range continually expanded by the boundless reach of electronic media.

But there is an even deeper connection, a bond that derives from the universal values America represents. More than a simple wishlist of desirable freedoms, at their core is the belief that these values have universal application, that they are inherent in individuals and peoples by right of humanity and not by the grace of the powerful and the unelected. They provide hope even for those populations which have never experienced hope.

The advancement of freedom has been a prominent component of American foreign policy since this country's inception. Given the nature of the American people, it is certain to remain so.

But in addition to genuine altruism, our promotion of freedom can have another purpose, namely as an element in the United States' geopolitical strategy.

Despite the laments and exasperations of the practitioners of Realpolitik regarding what they see as our simplistic and naïve images of the world, we haven't done so badly. That virtually the entire continent of Europe is free and secure today is largely due to America's powerful and beneficent embrace, one that stretches unbroken from the landings in Normandy to the present day.

The history of the last century taught us many lessons, one of the most important being that the desire for freedom we share with others can be a remarkably powerful weapon for undermining geopolitical threats. The prime example is the Soviet Union.

Decades of enormous effort on the part of the United States and the West aimed at containing and undermining the threat posed by the Soviet empire enjoyed considerable success. But it was only with the advent of democracy in Russia and the other nations of the Soviet prisonhouse that the communist regime was finally destroyed and with it the menace it posed to us and to the world as a whole. This should be a deep lesson for us, but it is one that curiously remains unlearned by many.

Candidates for the application of this lesson come readily to mind: the list of countries posing threats to the United States, such as Iraq, Iran, and North Korea, contains no democracies. All are repressive, all maintain their rule by coercion. Given the closed nature of these regimes, the conventional tools available to the

United States to affect the behavior of these and other regimes are frustratingly limited, often amounting to little more than a mix of sanctions, condemnation, and diplomatic isolation. Despite great effort on our part, each of these regimes continues its course toward the acquisition of weapons of mass destruction, holding out the frightening prospect of a vast increase in their ability to do harm to the United States and its interests.

An even greater challenge lies in the emergence of China.

China's rapidly growing strength cannot but have a profound impact on the international system. Were the government in Beijing to maintain its apparently zero-sum view of the world, China's influence could expand in East Asia and elsewhere only at the expense of that of the United States. Even more troubling is that the regime has consciously chosen to bolster its fading ideological legitimacy with an open appeal to a xenophobic nationalism.

Although China's emergence is likely to pose the single greatest strategic challenge the U.S. faces in the 21st century, our conventional tools for affecting its course, however, are quite modest.

But in our search for leverage against the regime's potentially destructive ambitions, we have overlooked our most powerful ally, namely the Chinese people. The source of that leverage is a shared goal—political freedom in China—and a common impediment: the regime in Beijing. Far from being merely a domestic concern, the issue of political freedom in China is directly relevant to the U.S. Were China to become a democracy, its adversarial impact on our influence and interests might well be minimized or even avoided altogether, and the prospect of genuine cooperation placed within reach. One need only compare our current relationships with democratic Germany, Japan, and Russia to those with their dictatorial predecessors to understand the transformative role democracy can play.

I have used the term "alliance" when speaking of our relationships with peoples around the world. I do not use the term lightly, nor is it merely a figure of speech. Although our global responsibilities require us to maintain a full complement of official interactions with regimes around the world, and even to cultivate good relations with them, we must remember that our true allies are the people they rule over. We are allies because we share a common aim, which is freedom. And we have a common opponent: oppressive regimes hostile to democracy.

Does this mean that we must cast our lot with the uncertain prospects of the oppressed around the world and forgo cooperation with their ruling regimes? Must we renounce traditional foreign policy goals, and even our own interests, in the name of revolution? Obviously, the answer is no. Adopting such a course would be profoundly foolish and would quickly prove to be unsustainable. Our interests require that we have allies, even close allies, whose hold on power does not rest on the consent of the governed. The first and enduring priority of American foreign policy is and must remain the promotion of the interests of the American people. Our desire to help others must not be confused with an obligation to do so. But neither should we ignore the necessity of maintaining our connections with the populations of those governments whose cooperation we need but whose tenure in power is not eternal.

This, then, is the purpose I would set for our public diplomacy and for our foreign policy as a whole: to engage our allies among the peoples of the world. This must include public pronouncements from the President and from the Congress that clearly state the long-term objectives of U.S. foreign policy. We must have good relations with the world's governments, but this must be complemented by our speaking past the regimes and the elites and directly to the people themselves.

Over a quarter century of life in Washington has taught me how difficult it is to change ingrained habits of thought. Still, I'm convinced that our system of government is flexible enough to accommodate new ideas and new approaches to old problems.

For all of America's enormous power, transforming the world is too heavy a burden to attempt alone. But we are not alone. The peoples of the world represent an enormous reservoir of strategic resources waiting to be utilized. The formula is a simple one: we can best advance our own interests not by persuading others to adopt our agenda but by helping them achieve their own freedom.

In so doing, we must always remember that though we have many vocal opponents, these are vastly outnumbered by the legions of our silent allies.

A public diplomacy rooted in a robust defense and promotion of American ideals is an idea whose time has come. In creating an activist public diplomacy of this type, we will be true to ourselves and to our convictions. For if we are to advance a foreign policy capable of leading the world to peace, security, freedom, and justice, we can do so only in partnership with the peoples of the world.

July 16, 2002

A Marshall Plan for the Middle East

The scene is a fearsome one: A region lacerated by violent conflict, its intractable hatreds amplified by ancient territorial disputes. Lands divided by barbed wire; a sea of refugees miserable in their camps; entire populations left to despair and destitution. This bleak picture could describe much of the Middle East today. But it also describes Europe in the aftermath of World War II.

Europe today lies peacefully in its cocoon of security, prosperity, and cooperation. The contrast with its former self and with the current Middle East could not be greater. But despite their profound differences, Europe's triumph over its fratricidal past offers realistic hope for a solution to the Middle Eastern quagmire.

In the aftermath of World War II, Europe was a devastated continent, where fear and revenge permeated the endless ruins. After a millennium of conflict and two world wars, Europe seemed destined to continue its endless series of bloodlettings. Instead, a miraculous change was to take place in these battered and cynical countries, a transformation set in motion and guided by the U.S.

Washington's assumption of a preeminent role in Europe's post-war recovery occurred by default but quickly took the form of a range of initiatives in many areas, including a comprehensive program of aid and economic reform that became known as the Marshall Plan. That Plan is justly famous as an example of far-sighted altruism, from feeding malnourished populations to rebuilding defeated enemies. But it also has proven to have been an excellent strategic investment for the United States as well. As a result of the wide-ranging programs implemented by the United States—with the Marshall Plan taking pride of place—Europe ceased to be an endemic source of conflict requiring massive U.S. intervention and has become a strong, stable, and immensely important partner, with the trans-Atlantic relationship comprising the foundation of the modern world.

The Marshall Plan consisted of more than merely shoveling money into outstretched hands, however. Among its many provisions was the requirement that the recipients embrace genuine and increasing cooperation among themselves, along with many other measures contributing to the broader goals of stability, peace, and political freedom. Grudging at first, cooperation was eventually made routine and gradually, haltingly transformed attitudes between historical adversaries. Institutions established to coordinate this assistance laid the groundwork for the creation of today's European Union. Without the U.S. to preside over this decades-long effort, to nudge and push along the reluctant participants, and to provide an unquestioned security to all, it is extremely doubtful that Europe would ever have emerged from the prison of its past.

A similarly irenic future for the Middle East may be too ambitious to contemplate, but a dramatic improvement need not be ruled out. The conflict is a many-sided one, but any prospect for a stable peace must include addressing the region's profound economic needs. Coupled with other measures regarding security and political matters, the promise of a Marshall Plan for the Middle East would be a powerful incentive to the adversaries to moderate their disputes and brave an initial wisp of cooperation that might eventually grow to significant proportions.

As with Europe, the prerequisites for a broader peace would include an elaborate array of measures to be adopted by all parties, including the establishment of the full complement of normal relations. These include mutual recognition, full diplomatic relations, economic and trade links, border crossings, and so forth. Over time, the habits of cooperation might put down lasting roots, even if mutual love were to remain forever out of reach.

A key difference from Europe's Marshall Plan would be the source of the funding. At the end of World War II, the U.S. possessed virtually the only economy not devastated by war. Today, however, Europe, Japan, and the wealthy countries of the region, such as Saudi Arabia and Kuwait, must contribute their share. But the U.S. must first set the plan in motion.

To that end, the House International Relations Committee begins hearings this week to address the shape and content of a Marshall Plan for the Middle East; its potential role as part of an overall effort to bring peace, stability, and prosperity to the region; and how we might best work with our allies in the Middle East, Europe, and elsewhere to make it a reality.

Peace in the Middle East: An unrealistic dream? The experience of Europe suggests otherwise. It is not within the power of the United States to impose a peace in the Middle East; that responsibility lies with the peoples and governments of the region. But assuming that they possess the necessary will, we can greatly assist their efforts, especially by changing the frozen, zero-sum calculations hobbling mind-sets throughout the region. As it was in Europe, the U.S. remains the only, the indispensable catalyst for lasting change on the battleground known as the Middle East.

February 11, 2003

The Pathology of Success

We meet at a time of great peril and great opportunity. The peril is obvious: aggressive regimes—armed with weapons of mass destruction, uncontrolled by any domestic political constraints, and linked to international terrorist networks in a shadow world of malice where the murder of innocents is considered a noble vocation. These threaten the very possibility of order in world affairs. In Iraq, the world's fifty-eight-year experiment with collective security is being put to the supreme test. If Iraq is permitted to defy twelve years of United Nations resolutions demanding its disarmament, then that fifty-eight-year experiment in collective security will be, for all intents and purposes, over. In enforcing the will of the UN as expressed most recently in Resolution 1441, the United States and its allies are upholding the minimum conditions for world order. Let us hope that Iraqi disarmament can be enforced with the united support of the Security Council. But let us make certain that effective and decisive enforcement takes place—by what the President has called a "coalition of the willing," if necessary.

This peril also contains, in my view, a great opportunity. The opportunity is to recast the politics of a turbulent region of the world, so that opportunities for real stability are created. What we often call "stability" in the Middle East has been, for the past half-century, the most volatile instability. The world cannot live with this instability much longer. It threatens world peace. It threatens the global economy. And, as the bitter lesson of 9-11 taught us, the instability of the Middle East can now reach around the globe and directly threaten the security of the people of the United States.

America is often said to be a "hyperpower," yet our actions are repeatedly frustrated by an endless train of objections and obstacles. America has fought distant wars to defend whole continents from a succession of aggressors, but the beneficiaries of the safety we have ensured often devote their energies to impeding our efforts to help others. We shoulder burdensome responsibilities for the benefit of the entire globe, but too often we must do so alone.

Americans are rightly puzzled by this and by what appears to many to be ingratitude, and even hostility, on the part of friends and allies. We see our own motives as noble and believe this fact to be self-evident. We are not an imperial power coldly focused on the subjugation of others or on securing some narrow advantage for ourselves. Instead, we are frequently moved to action by the plight of others, often losing sight of our own self-interest in our zeal to make the world right. None can doubt that, for over half a century, we have employed our power in the service of making the world safe, peaceful, and prosperous to the extent of our ability to do so.

It is true that we are not motivated by altruism alone. We cannot be, for we have a responsibility for our own welfare that cannot be delegated to others, not even the UN. But altruism has always been woven into the policies of our republic. Given the nature of our fundamental principals and beliefs, it cannot be otherwise.

How is it then that we do so much for so many others and yet have to plead for support? Why is it always so difficult to enlist others in causes from which all benefit? Why do we carry global responsibilities, yet others feel no need to assume a share of the collective burden?

While it may be tempting to resent our allies and others for what appears as cynical and perverse behavior, the truth is that this puzzle is one of our own making. It is in fact the product of our very success in remaking the world. It is the defining trait of what may be termed "The Pathology of Success."

Great success often prompts a corresponding envy in others, and our occasional humbling is a rich and guilty pleasure often indulged in by friends and foes alike. That is the principal reason Castro is celebrated by a spectrum of leaders stretching from Third World dictators to our NATO allies. The former take heart from the fact that he has defied the power of the United States and survived. For the latter, cultivating ties with our declared enemy has long been an easy and risk-free way for them to demonstrate their independence from us, even as we remain pledged to their defense.

Dependence can also evoke a corrosive resentment that can slumber in the deepest layers, even with friends. This is especially true among those whose ambitions are not matched by their capabilities and who are reminded of their less-than-central role in the world by what they believe is our failure to sufficiently consult with them regarding our own decisions.

Ultimately, however, these explanations do not adequately describe the phenomenon.

The fundamental problem is simply this: Given our strength, the urgency of our many concerns, and our willingness to proceed alone, if necessary, we have liberated others from the responsibility of defending their own interests, to say nothing of any responsibility for the collective interests of the West. Many would watch the night descend on others in far-away countries of which they know little without any feeling that perhaps they should do something to halt it and that not doing so might be a perilous option. Far from assisting, they might even devote their energies to preventing others from doing something.

The vast extent of our success has created the equivalent of a moral hazard, the dangers of which we are encountering with increasing frequency.

The clearest example of this in the international system is Europe. In the 1,500 years following the fall of the Roman Empire, Europe was a warring continent, where suspicion and betrayal were forces of nature, and peace but an uncertain interlude between conflicts. This world was upended by the United States. In the aftermath of World War II, with Europe devastated and still smoldering from ancient hatreds, the United States assumed a dominant role in all aspects, reviving prostrate economies with unprecedented aid, shoring up weak democracies, insisting on ever-closer cooperation between former enemies, establishing the institutions by which a unity of purpose came into being, weaving the whole into a community.

And embracing it all, the United States provided an absolute guarantee of safety. Problems shrank to the scale of daily life; dangers evaporated into abstract metaphors. Sheltered by American power, the hostilities of the untamed world beyond became remote, and then imaginary.

This unearned inheritance did not require any of the beneficiaries to assume any risk, take on oppressive burdens, acknowledge their debt, or do anything other than focus on a pursuit of self-interest. They remained safe regardless of what they did or did not do. The natural state of the world was transformed from one ruled by fear and competition to one of safety and peace. And, like Nature, it required no effort on the part of man to bring it into being. Instead of hard choices of war and peace, it was more akin to selecting from an a la carte menu, guided only by one's tastes and momentary preferences. It was a profoundly false view of the world, but can we fault those who were raised in this cocoon of our making?

We may blame others for their short-sightedness, but it is we who have distorted their perceptions of reality. It is we who have created a beneficent, but artificial, environment so secure that its beneficiaries believe it to be self-sustaining. They feel neither need nor obligation to do anything to defend their interests, to secure those of the West, to ensure order rather than disorder in the world beyond their garden.

Seen from this perspective, the United States becomes not the protector of the West in Iraq and elsewhere, but its tormentor, its power not the source of security but of disorder, a blundering and myopic Goliath whose misguided efforts are threatening to all. If only the U.S. were to desist, they say, we would once again be serene. The image is so inverted that one can almost hear the distant musical strains of the "The World Turned Upside Down."

To a lesser degree, a similar situation prevails in East Asia, where the conquest, oppression, fear, and war of the past have given way to a prosperous, cooperative, secure system of free states, one which I am pleased to say is populated by an increasing number of democracies. The United States played a direct hand in bringing about many of these historic changes, but its most profound contribution was to create and defend a nurturing and secure environment in which this transformation could take place. And we have defended it with tens of thousands of American dead and uncounted billions in treasure.

But here again, we see the dangerous abdication of responsibility that has arisen out of the artificial environment we have established. All problems have become America's responsibility, while others, even those with more immediate interests than ours, stand on the sidelines offering passive encouragement or vocal abuse.

We see the absurdity of this situation in the current crisis regarding North Korea. Somehow, this problem is judged by both ourselves and others to be ours, and almost ours alone.

It is not seen as a challenge to be met by the countries of East Asia, which watch to see the course we will take in order to tack to the prevailing winds. It is not assumed to be that of the rest of the world, which distractedly wonders why the U.S. has not yet resolved this far-away problem. Nor is it that of China, whose influence in Pyongyang is paramount and without whose assistance the regime would quickly collapse.

It is not even that of South Korea, which we liberated at great cost in young lives and have defended from conquest for over half a century, but where we are now openly accused of being the unwelcome source of that peninsula's misfortunes.

The familiarity of these problems, however, obscures a deeper danger. We have entered a new and more threatening century, one in which the civilized world will be under increasing assault from the forces of terror and dismemberment. These forces cannot be dissuaded by reason or by the paying of tribute. We are certain to discover that our ability to hold back the rising tide of disorder is finite and that we cannot by ourselves alone defend the West from those who even now are plotting our destruction. Others must now take up their long-ignored responsibility and assume their place in the line, not only for their own sake but for us all.

We cannot wait for disaster to awaken them from their dreams of summer. Instead, we must expose them to the dangers of a rough reality, for only with the ensuing abrasions is there hope that their comforting illusions can be worn away. The alarm has already begun to sound, but, as yet, it remains unheard.

Justice demands that I make an exception to my reproach, and that exception is Britain. Our ties are deep. Britain remains the mother country even for those Americans whose ancestors never touched British soil. We are joined not merely by common interests, but by a shared recognition that, if our world is to be preserved, we have no option but to accept our duty. For Britain, the term "ally" is simply insufficient. We are, in truth, partners. In saying this, I do not mean to fail to express my admiration of the dozens of countries who have bravely offered their support.

We have made much of the world a welcoming one for all the wondrous things to which mankind has aspired over the centuries. But we have also established it on a perilous foundation, one that permits its citizens a fatal irresponsibility.

The fault is ours, not theirs. It is we who have mistakenly allowed others to learn a false and dangerous lesson. To believe that the peace and safety of the West, the product of centuries of effort, will maintain itself, that order need not be wrested from the storms and chaos that surround us, to believe that our world is not a fragile thing, is to risk everything. We have in fact made our world safe in the disastrous belief that others need not share a part of the collective burden, that there is no burden to be borne at all.

We may, in fact, be risking everything. Let me quote the warning by the philosopher, Ortega y Gasset: If you want to make use of the advantages of civilization, but are not prepared to concern yourself with the upholding of civilization—you are done...Just a slip, and when you look around, everything has vanished into air.

It is one of the paradoxes of our time that the American people, who have never dreamed dreams of empire, should find themselves given a unique responsibility for the course of world history. As you said so eloquently during your recent speech at Davos, Mr. Secretary, Americans did not go into the world in the 20th Century for self-aggrandizement, but rather for the liberation of others—asking of those others only a small piece of ground in which to bury our dead, who gave their lives for the freedom of men and women they never knew or met. Now, in these first, determinative years of the 21st Century, we are being challenged to such large tasks again. We did not ask to be so challenged, but we dare not let the challenge go unanswered.

Causes Won
Lost, or
Otherwise

A man on the move, surrounded by the people moving him.

I say "otherwise" because, as every political veteran knows, most causes meet with only partial victory or partial defeat. There is within the American political system an enormous degree of muddling through, rather than clear-cut triumphs or absolutely crushing losses. Why that is so, I can only speculate. Perhaps our federal system of government cushions ideological outcomes, so that what wins in some places does not carry the day elsewhere. Perhaps the very unwieldiness of our bicameral legislatures, especially our supersized House of Representatives, grinds down some of the sharper edges of competing approaches. Be that as it may, my long experience within that system has given me a profound appreciation for the handiwork of Mr. Madison and his fellow Framers. Because we continue to operate within their institutional framework, it usually takes a long time for anyone's pet cause to effect significant policy change—and even longer for such changes to permeate the social fabric of the nation.

In politics, there is no cause as risky as a sure thing. A case in point was the attempt, at the start of the Clinton Administration, to nationalize American medicine. No quibbles about the wording, please: for anyone who had to plow through the details of what was popularly referred to as Hillarycare knows that it was nothing short of total government takeover of health care. At its outset, it seemed the proverbial juggernaut, certain to be passed by liberal majorities in House and Senate, with the benign blessing of most of the country's media, academic, and religious establishment. Its inevitability crashed head-on into a more powerful force: Truth, in the hands of people who knew how to use it. In the House, Majority Leader Dick Armey's team at the Republican Conference put together a suddenly famous chart, graphically showing the public what a nightmare of regulation and controls Hillarycare would be. A magisterial speech, a manifesto really, drafted by a member of my Policy

Committee staff and distributed to all our guys by Newt Gingrich, energized our rank and file to take the offensive in town hall meetings and media appearances. I contributed an article, in the conservative paper *Human Events*, exposing the way taxpayer-funded abortion was required throughout the plan, thereby dampening enthusiasm for it in certain church quarters and among some Democrats.

The Administration's proposal collapsed under the weight of our truth-telling. Another sure thing bit the dust, just as had, in earlier years, several ill-conceived welfare plans, federalized child care, the Equal Rights Amendment, the Consumer Protection Agency, Common Situs Picketing, and a host of other liberal causes whose time came, and went, because conservatives stood their ground.

I hope the speeches in this section stand on solid ground. The issues they address are, for the most part, still being debated. Some are divisive, as indeed they should be when they address the core values of a far from united country. If there is one constant that runs through them all, it is the rule of law. That concept—the idea that our disagreements with one another should be fought out within the parameters of a generally fair and impartial legal system—has underlain my entire adult career, both as an attorney, a state legislator, and a Member of Congress.

Today, however, that concept is in disrepute. At the country's most prestigious law schools, aspiring attorneys are indoctrinated with quite a different view. They are taught that law is simply an instrument of power employed by the ruling class to protect its holdings and advance its interests. They are the leftist version of Cornelius Vanderbilt, demanding, at the height of the Victorian Gilded Age, "What do I care about the law? Hain't I got the power?" In that context, respect for the law is absurd. All that matters is gaining control of the legal system, to supplant one set of interests with your own. And the best way to do that? Control the courts by advancing your fellow-thinkers and by blocking those who do not share your point of view. There, in highly condensed form, you have the history of the federal judiciary for the last half-century or more.

Speaking of the judiciary gives me an excuse to recall Justice Charles Evans Hughes' observation that lawyers spend much of their time shoveling smoke. I hope the following speeches do not fall into that category. The first of them concerns the effort to ensure protection of the symbol of our nation, the American flag; and I have adapted its title for this entire volume (with apologies to Richard Whalen, whose book about the Nixon Administration was *Catch the Falling Flag*). This is one issue that is widely understood, though I hope my remarks may clarify certain aspects of the debate. I still think a constitutional amendment is called for; but it's worth noting that the campaign to protect the flag, while thwarted legislatively, seems to have been operationally successful. Recall the pro-immigration rallies of 2006, and how quickly their organizers moved to submerge the various Latin American banners in a sea of Stars and Stripes. Likewise, today's protestors against the war in Iraq wave the flag rather than desecrate it. It seems an important lesson has been learned and that, with the passage of time, flag-burning, while still legal, has become as anachronistic as love beads. Perhaps the legal status of Old Glory is one of those causes that can be considered "otherwise."

Some conservatives were less than enthusiastic about our constitutional amendment to protect the flag, and I do respect their rationale. They argued, quite rightly, that the problems with the Supreme Court's jurisprudence concerning freedom of speech were much more deeply rooted, and the flag-burning controversy was but the tip of an iceberg. As George Will and others pointed out at the time, the free speech provision of the First Amendment was intended by its Framers to protect political speech, which is to say, public discourse about public things. But a series of Court decisions—proclamations, really—had radically redefined "speech" to mean self-expression, even topless dancing. It would have been ideal if, instead of addressing only the flag issue, we could have gone so far as to restore the true meaning of the First Amendment. But that was not in the offing, which is why, to the dismay of his admirers, even Justice Antonin Scalia had voted to strike down an earlier flag-protection statute. Caught in the web of the Court's prior distortion of "speech," he saw little choice in the matter. The whole episode should be a lesson in what I propose to call constitutional environmentalism: When a judicial wellspring is intellectually tainted at its source, the subsequent stream of decisions can only spread the pollution.

The same can be said of badly written legislation. My favorite case in point is the Independent Counsel statute, the law which was wielded so recklessly by those who were determined to thwart President Reagan's eventually successful effort to prevent a Marxist takeover of Central America. In the media shorthand of the day, it was called the Iran-Contra Affair. At the risk of reopening old wounds, after this introduction, I offer for your consideration my final argument in defense of those who had been accused of official misconduct. Liberals said the heart of the matter was abuse of power by individuals in the employ of the President, if not by Mr. Reagan himself. My contention, now as then, is that the horrific abuse of authority was committed by the independent counsel assigned to look into the matter. At the cost of tens of millions of dollars, honorable men had been ground into penury and disgrace in the course of an open-ended witch hunt.

The independent counsel statute, enacted as a Watergate-era "reform," virtually guaranteed the repetition of those abuses. So when its authorization was expiring in 1993, I proposed amendments that would have ensured fairness, fiscal responsibility, and timeliness in future investigations—as well as applying the law to Congress itself! I pleaded with House Democrats to at least consider their party's own interest, now that they controlled the Executive Branch, lest future independent counsels should be turned loose upon members of the Clinton Administration the way they were set upon President Reagan's appointees. They refused, perhaps because any concession would have seemed like a retroactive repudiation of the Iran-Contra prosecutions. So they reauthorized the law as it stood, thereby setting in place the legal snare that would eventually entrap Mr. Clinton and others on his team. There is cold comfort in saying, "I told you so," but I did. In this case, my cause turned out to be a loss for just about everybody.

Another of my causes dealt with asset forfeiture, something with which, believe me, you do not want to get involved. (You wouldn't want to wade through a speech about it either.) But you should at least know these basics. In reaction to the drug tsunami that hit our country in the 1970s and 1980s, the Congress enacted legislation that had the effect of allowing law enforcement officials to seize a person's property on the untested suspicion that it was being used in an illegal enterprise. To reclaim the property, you would have to, in effect, prove your innocence; and even then, there was no guarantee you could recoup your losses. Yes, right here in America. I eventually succeeded in convincing my colleagues to take corrective action and, in one of those dramatic closed-door meetings that usually occur only in movies about the Congress, hammered out a deal with Senator Orrin Hatch, my counterpart in his role as Chairman of the Senate Judiciary Committee, and Janet Reno, President Clinton's Attorney General. So victory came in a quick meeting, but only after years of stubborn work—interviews, speeches, committee meetings, personal lobbying—on the issue. There must be a lesson in there somewhere.

On another front, I'm still looking for someone to take up my seemingly lost cause of combining the separate House and Senate Committees on Intelligence into a single joint committee. If that seems a mere bureaucratic detail, consider that it later became one of the key recommendations of the National Commission on Terrorist Attacks Upon the United States. While almost all of the 9/11 Commission's proposals have been implemented to one degree or another, this proposed change in the innermost workings of Congress has gone nowhere. Today, as during the many years when I labored on its behalf, the idea of a joint committee—an essential element in the modernization of our national security apparatus—runs up against certain powerful egos and even more powerful institutional vanities. May it not always be so.

The last two speeches in this section concern what are now referred to as "life issues," which is a much less jarring term than the word abortion. Even after all these years, thirty-four and counting, since the Supreme Court's decision in *Roe* v. *Wade*, that term is still so charged emotionally that it seems to sting the tongue as we utter it. No wonder that those who call themselves "pro-choice" prefer euphemisms like "termination of pregnancy." I know of no Terminator of Pregnancies who has ever hung out a shingle advertising himself as an "abortionist." That label is still a quasi-obscenity in the American vocabulary.

I will not repeat here the content of these speeches. Rather, I would like to return to my initial observation about the status of causes, especially causes of great magnitude. How should we, at this moment in our country's history, consider the pro-life cause, whatever our own views on abortion may be? Three decades ago, in the immediate aftermath of the *Roe* decision, it was thought a lost cause; all the best sort of people said so. Unfettered abortion rights were here to stay; the occasional pro-life amendment in Congress was a mere nuisance from an extremist faction on the sidelines of the future. To paraphrase Churchill's defiant retort to Hitler's threat to wring England's neck like a chicken: Some faction! Some nuisance! Today, most legal analysts expect that, if a single pro-*Roe* member of the Supreme Court is replaced with a jurist more respectful of the text of the Constitution, then *Roe* and all its malformed case progeny are doomed.

That may or may not happen anytime soon, especially in light of the vagaries of presidential elections and contested seats in the United State Senate. But odds are that it will indeed happen eventually. I am confident of the general thrust of the eventual outcome—or outcomes, because the task of restoring intellectual integrity to American jurisprudence after its systemic infection consequent upon *Roe* will require multiple decisions by the Supreme Court, as well as subsequent legal actions by both Congress and the states. In other words, it's going to be a big, messy fight for a long time; but over time, over most of America, there will be substantial legal protection for unborn children. While the degree of protection will, at least at first, vary from state to state, our national ethos, as expressed in federal law and policy, is going to tilt toward the pro-life view of things.

Remember, total victory is rare in American politics. And when it does come, total legal victory—as in the form of a Human Life Amendment to the Constitution—usually is attained only after its functional equivalent has already been secured. Thus, the Eighteenth Amendment to the Constitution was adopted only after most of the country, geographically, had already "gone dry." Likewise, the Nineteenth Amendment, establishing women's suffrage, was a capstone to the female enfranchisement that was already sweeping the states. The same can be said of the Twenty-Fourth Amendment, lowering the federal voting age from 21 to 18. None of this is reason for pro-lifers to abandon their original goal of amending the Constitution. It is, rather, a reason for them to take heart in all the little steps and peripheral advances that one day can simply be confirmed by a constitutional reaffirmation of pre-natal personhood. All of which sets the stage for the third item that follows, a speech I delivered at the National Right to Life Convention in 1987. It is obviously dated now and thus shows how much has changed in the last twenty years.

When the pro-life movement first began to focus on the atrocity known as partial-birth abortion, there were those who feared the tactic might backfire. They thought, rightly enough, that some pro-choice politicians would support a ban on that gruesome technique in order to appear moderate and more electable. The late Democratic Senator from New York, Daniel Patrick Moynihan, for example, famously denounced the procedure as "indistinguishable from infanticide." Many of his pro-choice colleagues followed his example, giving us supermajorities in the Congress to enact the current federal prohibition against scissors-in-the-baby's-head abortion. That law was struck down by several federal judges, who held that it conflicted with the abortion liberty enshrined in *Roe*. Now the Supreme Court has overturned those negative rulings. Indeed, the five justices who upheld the constitutionality of the partial-birth ban did so while I was still revising this introduction. In the process, they turned what had been merely my prediction into accomplished fact.

This is more than just a legal victory, and its outcome holds an important lesson for pro-life activists. The partial-birth issue was the best educational opportunity the pro-life movement ever had. After all, before you can convince someone of your point of view, you first have to get their attention; and nothing got the attention of the American people better than the graphic barbarity of a partial-birth procedure. Which leads me to include hereafter, as a final addendum, the comments I made when the House of Representatives debated this matter. I do so confident that, someday, when this volume is gathering dust in some library and occasional browsers wonder who this Hyde fellow was, the sad subject of these last remarks will be universally considered a tragic departure from all that was noble and heroic and worthy in our nation's past.

June 21, 1990

Catch the Burning Flag

One of the least pleasant aspects of this controversy is the demagoguery on both sides of the issue. Neither side should demean the issue by questioning the other's motives. To my conservative friends, I say a very respectable case can be made in opposition to amending the Constitution to protect the American flag. After all, the fullest and freest speech, including expressive conduct, has much to recommend it; and no one's patriotism ought to be questioned if their best judgment is to oppose protecting the flag by amending the Constitution. By the same token, those of us who do support an amendment should not be denigrated as yahoos, cowards, mindless political animals, and worse—all by those who refuse to concede that a scholarly and cogent case can be made for the amendment.

I do not know which side of this debate deserves the credit for courage. I do not know if it takes more courage to vote against this constitutional amendment and incur the slings and arrows of some outraged veterans' organizations, or whether it takes more courage on our side to endure the slings and arrows of the media, which relentlessly condemns us as cultural lags and political pygmies for our alleged weakness in caving in to the populist patriotic notions of the American people.

But I will concede that this is a close call. This is not an easy amendment to vote on. The Supreme Court's decision concerning the flag, which this amendment would correct, was also a close call, a 5-to-4 decision, and so it is in many of our minds and many of our hearts. We who support this amendment keep some very distinguished company. Among commentators, George Will and David Broder have stated their support, as have Chief Justice Rehnquist, Justice White, Justice O'Connor, Justice Stevens, former Chief Justice Earl Warren, and Justices Hugh Black and Abe Fortas—not to mention Judge Robert Bork and many others. All have expressed the conviction that the flag is constitutionally protectable from burning. Indeed, to say we are powerless to protect the flag from defilement is to confess an impotence that would have astonished the founders of this Republic.

It is not the text of the First Amendment we seek to amend. Freedom of speech is untouched by this amendment. Our quarrel is with the Court's interpretation of "speech," which radically expands the meaning of a constitutional provision originally intended to safeguard actual political discourse. As Justice Rehnquist has said, flag burning does not express an idea. It is a grunt designed not to communicate but to antagonize.

I wish we did not have to amend the Constitution to achieve the desired result. We are driven to this extremity by the decision of the Court. When the Supreme Court makes a mistake, it is the responsibility of the people's body to propose to the States a correction, and that is all we are doing. We are proposing a correction. It is disingenuous—or at best, historically ignorant—to assert, as many journalists and politicians have, that this would be the first time in 200 years that we would amend the Bill of Rights. The fact is, Congress has reversed an errant Supreme Court by amendment four times in our history.

For starters, the Thirteenth Amendment and the Fourteenth Amendment in 1865 and 1867 both amended an 1857 decision of the Court, in the *Dred Scott* case, which had been based on a deplorable misinterpretation of the Fifth Amendment. In 1895, the Court's decision in *Pollock* v. *Farmers Loan and Trust Company* declared the federal income tax unconstitutional, in a 5 to 4 decision that was reversed in 1913 by the Sixteenth Amendment. In *Oregon* v. *Mitchell*, another 5 to 4 decision in 1970, the Court invalidated an act of Congress that gave 18-year-olds the right to vote in state as well as federal elections. Congress reversed that decision with the Twenty-Sixth amendment in 1971. *Chisholm* v. *Georgia*, in 1793, was reversed by the Eleventh Amendment in 1798, which protected the States from citizen suits brought in federal courts without congressional authority.

So Court decisions based on the Bill of Rights have indeed been reversed by constitutional amendments. Those amendments, like the one we are debating today, did not amend the Bill of Rights, but merely corrected a decision of the Court.

And please, those of you who fell all over yourselves to support the Equal Rights Amendment must have understood that it amended the Bill of Rights because it claimed that the word "person" in the Fifth Amendment did not include women. "No person shall be deprived of equal protection under the law." "No person shall be deprived of due process of law." You must have held that "person" was devoid of female content because you insisted on the gender-specific ERA, and that was all right. But do not say that there is something unchangeable about the Bill of Rights when you yourselves have sought to change it.

By the way, the currently proposed Civil Rights Act of 1990 seeks to reverse four Supreme Court cases. So we are not really averse to doing that, are we?

Should we protect the flag? What is so special about this flag? It is unique, sui generis, in a class by itself, nothing else like it. It is transcendent. It rises above the political swamps in which we live and work, and it serves as a symbol of our unity and our community as a country. It symbolizes America as nothing else does. The uniqueness of this flag is why we want to treat it differently from everything else.

Not all expressive conduct is protected by the Bill of Rights. Perjury is not protected. Copyright and trademark laws protect certain language and punish other usages of it. Libel and slander, obscenity, classified information, verbal agreements in restraint of trade, contemptuous speech in a courtroom—there are all sorts of exceptions to absolute free speech. Moreover, if I have a $20 bill, I cannot burn it. If I stand here and burn it, I am violating a federal law. But I can burn a flag. That is an interesting anomaly.

Let me state the obvious: Our flag represents for all the world the truths so majestically announced in the Declaration of Independence. For all of us, it is not an opinion, it is beyond debate, that every member of the human family is created equal and endowed by their Creator with inalienable rights. Our rights are an endowment, not an achievement. That belief is what unites us. We are Poles, and we are Greeks. We are blacks and whites, Mormons and Catholics and Irish. We are everything. We lack the cultural homogeneity of a China, a France, or a Japan. And yet we are united in those marvelous gifts, those endowments from our Creator. Which may be why the symbol for America in deaf language is linking your fingers and moving your arms in a circle.

This is the unanimity that we share: that "to secure these rights, governments are instituted among men, deriving their just authority from the consent of the governed." Can we agree on that much? Can we not get a symbol for that agreement and elevate it and say that it unites us as one nation, indivisible, with liberty and justice for all? I think so, and that is why the VFW and the American Legion and the kids who pledge allegiance to the flag look to us to preserve and protect it from desecration. A Member of the House swears to defend the Constitution once every two years. But every day you can pledge allegiance. The two are not incompatible.

The ghosts of Jefferson and Madison have been summoned here to oppose this amendment. I wish that whoever has the power to summon ghosts would summon them from Flanders Fields and have them come here and tell Members what they mean when they say, "We will not sleep if you do not keep faith with us."

I want to tell Members something personal. I am one who despised the Vietnam Memorial. I thought it was a depressing funereal ditch. I thought it lacked inspiration, a recognition of the nobility of the sacrifice made, and I really disliked it. However, I was absolutely wrong. I go there and stand there and those names absolutely overwhelm me. Every one of them, a human being who loved this country as much as others do, and as much as you and I do. Then, imagine above that, another monument with the names of those who lost their lives in Korea, and in World War II, World War I. Go on back, all the way to the War of 1812 and the Revolutionary War. All of those names are people to whom we owe so much. We owe it to them to keep faith with their sacrifice.

It is little enough to have the symbol of what they died for, the values they died for, special and protected. This is one more struggle in the culture war that has been raging in America since Vietnam. Those who are shocked by the excesses of the counterculture—the pornography and obscenity that inundate our entertainment industry, the drug abuse, the AIDS epidemic, the staggering abortion rate—they view flag burning as one more slap in the face, one more calculated insult to the millions of veterans who risked their lives in defense of the nation. So let Members of this House take the flag out of the gutter where some have dragged it. For this is an opportunity, not to get even with some creeps, but to say there are transcendent values that are important to every American, that unify Americans, that bring us together as one nation under God. Is that not important? Indeed it is important, and when the flag is falling, we have to pick it up. That does not, as some contend, shoot a hole in the Bill of Rights. It exalts the Bill of Rights.

Remember, when everything is permitted, and nothing is forbidden, we are heeding the ghost of Robespierre, not Jefferson or Madison. We do not understand freedom if we do not understand responsibility. For every right, there is a correlative duty. But though we have a Bill of Rights; we lack a Bill of Duties. We have ten amendments that guarantee us all kinds of rights. How about one amendment that says we have a duty, not to respect the flag or to love it, but just not to destroy it or defile it? Is that too much to ask, one duty? The law, it is said, is a teacher, and it should be a teacher here.

Henry Adams, when he looked at the cathedral at Chartres, said it embodied the noblest aspirations of mankind, the reaching up to infinity. I do not say that the flag is a sacred symbol in the spiritual or religious sense, but I do say it is a unique symbol, and too many people have paid for it with their blood. Too many have marched behind it, too many have slept in their caskets beneath it, too many kids and parents and widows have held this star-spangled triangle as the last remembrance of their most precious son, father, or husband. Too many to have this flag demeaned. For all their sakes, can we not protect the transcendent symbol of all that is good in our country?

Listen, the flag is falling. I ask Members to catch the falling flag and raise it back up. That will not tear down the Constitution. It will elevate us all to being worthy of the great country we live in.

November 13, 1987

The Iran-Contra Affair

One unanticipated benefit of the Iran-Contra hearings was the surprising emergence of so many strict constructionists among members of the Joint Investigating Committee. It is heartening to see the ranks of those devoted to law and order increasing, notwithstanding the selectivity of their devotion.

In earlier days, we were conditioned to favor appeals to "the higher law" over mere statutory expressions, depending on who made the appeal and the degree of left-ward tilt to their cause.

We have seen high-minded demonstrators trespass on military installations, splash animal blood on draft records, illegally picket within 500 feet of the South African Embassy, conduct sit-ins to obstruct C.I.A. university recruitment, and deliberately violate our immigration laws to provide sanctuary to a chosen few.

These acts of civil and criminal disobedience are routinely applauded by many who turn a cold shoulder, a blind eye and a deaf ear towards such appeals when made by, for example, Fawn Hail on behalf of her former boss, Lt. Col. Oliver North.

Ms. Hall's testimony that "sometimes you have to go above the written law . . ." has been much remarked in the press, but we are less often reminded that she was echoing Thomas Jefferson, who on September 20, 1810 wrote to John Colvin:

> A strict observance of the written law is doubtless *one* of the high duties of a good citizen, but it is not *the highest*. The laws of necessity, of self preservation, of saving our country when in danger, are of higher obligation. To lose our country, by a scrupulous adherence to written law, would be to lose the law itself, with life, liberty and property and all those who are enjoying them with us; thus absurdly sacrificing the end to the means.* (*Writings of Thomas Jefferson*, n. 28 at p. 279.)

The selective availability of "the higher law" is but one of the anomalies underscored by these hearings, and has particular relevance to any study of the scope and applicability of the various Boland Amendments.

A dominant theme of these hearings has been vigorous condemnation of those who allegedly violated the letter or the spirit of the Boland Amendments, or who lied to Congress or were not forthcoming in their testimony about Central American policy. The rationale for these transgressions—the need for secrecy to protect lives, the sensitivity of negotiations with Iran about hostages, combined with the notorious inability of Congress to keep a secret—were summarily rejected by most of the committee's members. We were regularly reminded of some bedrock propositions, including the President's duty under the Constitution to see that the laws are faithfully executed, that we are a government of laws and not of men (most especially in this bicentennial year) and that the end cannot justify the means.

These propositions—true enough—deserve a less facile application to the complex events involved in these hearings. All of us at some time confront conflicts—between rights and duties, between choices that are evil and less evil, and one hardly exhausts moral imagination by labeling every untruth and every deception an outrage.

In assessing how helpful the axiom is that "the end doesn't justify the means," I suggest consideration of the dilemma facing President Harry S. Truman on August 6, 1945.

Four months earlier, the invasion of Okinawa cost 151,000 American and Japanese lives. The resistance was suicidal, and the Joint Chiefs of Staff believed if this World War was to end, Japan itself would have to be invaded. The best military estimates anticipated a loss of one million American lives and no one could guess how many more million Japanese lives. The President had no options that could be called good, but the stark choices before him required a decision: to drop the atomic bomb on Hiroshima (and, indeed, Nagasaki) and thus end the war or to invade the Japanese homeland at a cost of untold millions of lives.

We all know Truman's decision, and for myself I believe it was the right one. But to those who think it was morally wrong and seek to indict Mr. Truman, I suggest, rather, they blame those in the Japanese government who forced this decision on him.

What has this to do with the Iran Contra affair? The circumstances and the actors are different but the moral dilemma is the same—or, as Lt. Col. North put it, "Lies or Lives."

Former Virginia Governor Charles Robb correctly summarized Congress' vacillating Nicaraguan Contra policy when he called it "playing with people's lives." New York Times correspondent James Le Moyne echoed that sentiment when he wrote recently that ". . . it is difficult not to conclude that it has been hypocritical, immoral and deeply damaging to the United States to send men to kill and to die for six years on half promises and sporadic assistance." Le Moyne concluded his October 4, 1987 article in the New York Times magazine with these observations by Donald Castillo, an ex-Sandinista who Le Moyne believes is "one of the Contras' most able political analysts: 'You North Americans have great values, but you need to learn to define and apply them . . . you have been generous to us—and you have also utilized and manipulated us as part of your domestic political agenda . . . But have you been aware that you're playing with the life and blood of a people and a country?' "

To those many who grew impatient with we few who insisted on discussing policy, I suggest that a fundamental reason for our differing perspectives on the purpose of these hearings may be the differing view we take towards the seriousness of the threat that Marxism-Leninism poses to peace, freedom, security and prosperity in the world. Those of us who not only take this threat seriously but also try to do something about it are often considered to exercise a "cold war mentality." This is a grave sin indeed in the liberal catechism. But our view of the urgency of the situation was well stated by Professor George McKenna of the City College of New York who wrote in the *New York Times* of June 5, 1987:

> "While Congress fiddles, the world burns. In the 1960's there were four openly proclaimed Marxist-Leninist regimes in the third world; today there are 16. Two Soviet client states are right at our doorstep, and they are working relentlessly to add another four to the Soviet fold: El Salvador, Guatemala, Honduras and Costa Rica. The Reagan Administration's 'crime' is that it tried to stop this process, just as the Roosevelt Administration tried to stop the expansion of another evil empire in the summer of 1940."

There are other contentious issues these hearings have emphasized—none more important than the proper constitutional roles of the President and the Congress in the formulation and execution of foreign policy. Senator George J. Mitchell of Maine and I have exchanged a series of letters on this subject, which I characterize as the struggle between the Congressional supremacists and the Presidential monarchists. Actually neither characterization is accurate, as each has a vital role which cannot exclude the other. But defining these boundaries is (to use Simon Bolivar's phrase) like plowing in the sea. Nonetheless a better understanding of the President's constitutional authority and that of Congress is essential if we are to ever develop and manage a successful foreign policy, regain the confidence of our allies and deserve the respect of our adversaries. The renewed focus on this "invitation to struggle" is one of the positive things to emerge from these hearings.

I will not burden these views with the arguments and citations I have made in my correspondence with Senator Mitchell, except to assert my general conclusion that the Founding Fathers intended to vest the general control of foreign affairs in the President—subject of course to the specific checks set forth in the Constitution. Citing *United States* v. *Curtiss-Wright Export Corp.* 299 U.S. 304, 319 (1936), the Tower Commission's report correctly asserted: "Whereas the ultimate power to formulate domestic policy resides in the Congress, the primary responsibility for the formulation and implementation of national security policy falls on the President." (PV-1)

There have been many elements of unreality about these hearings. But the most serious breach of reality has had to do with why we held them in the first place. What was it, really, that brought us to create these select committees? Some will argue that it was a concern for Constitutional process; and well we should have been concerned. But to leave the matter there obscures what seems to me a crucial substantive issue, a real and deep division that has led to this exercise.

That division, to be simple, accurate and blunt, can be stated thus: there are Members of the House and Senate who do not believe that communism in Central America is a grave threat to peace and freedom that requires an active and vigorous response from the United States; there are Members who concede the threat in the abstract, but wish to do little about it beyond talking; and there are Members who acknowledge the threat and wish to challenge it, forthrightly, through the variety of instruments proposed by the National Bipartisan Commission on Central America.

In real political life, the first two categories of Members—those who see little or no threat, and those who see the threat but cannot gather themselves to challenge it—work together. Their alliance, as curious as it may seem in the abstract, is what accounts for the baroque dance of the Boland Amendments. This strange alliance between the unbelieving and the believing-but-unwilling has made a mockery of our foreign policy: we have had one policy one year, and another policy the next.

This has reinforced the tendency of insecure Latin American leaders to say one thing in private and another in public. This strange alliance of political convenience and/or confusion has further strengthened anti-anticommunism here at home. One shudders to think of what it has taught the Soviets.

Whether one traces this triple division to that all-purpose whipping boy, "Vietnam," or whether one finds longer historical lines feeding it, it remains a desperately debilitating fact of our national life. When members of the Congress of the United States look at the same situation and see radically different things—or, seeing the same thing, differ utterly on what, if anything, is to be done about it—we are in far deeper trouble than the issue of Constitutional propriety.

My side of the argument—those who both see the communist threat in Central America and wish to address it through economic, humanitarian, and security assistance to that region's democrats—carries its share of the blame for the impasse we have reached. We have somehow failed to convince those who see the threat we see that there are ways to address that threat which serve the ends of peace, freedom, and justice. Our failure to make this argument successfully—a failure, I say in all candor, that has plagued the White House as well—has created circumstances in which those who neither see nor wish to act have co-opted some of their more prescient colleagues. The result has been the kind of schizophrenic Congressional policy that we have been enduring these past months.

Meanwhile, whatever its own failures of persuasion, the Executive has had to act. At the other end of Pennsylvania Avenue, there is precious little of the luxury of ambiguity. One must act (always, one hopes and prays, wisely), for not to act, in this world, is itself an action. Sins of omission, according to classic moral theory, can be as grave as sins of commission. The Executive has not sinned, largely, on the omission side of the ledger (save in its unwillingness to make its case to the country in and out of season). Conversely, we have seen ample evidence of the ways in which the Executive has acted that can be legitimately criticized. But there is a luxury we indulge here. For the sake of Constitutional propriety, we must, on occasion, indulge it—this luxury of restrospective wisdom. But it should be a rare indulgence. It can lead to policy confusion and indeed paralysis. Indulge the luxury of retrospective wisdom too promiscuously, and we inevitably fall into sins of omission—which can be as bad, indeed, worse, than the sins of commission. Neville Chamberlain was a good and decent man, and an ambiguist. The Czechoslovaks paid the price for his sins of omission in 1938. His countrymen paid for the next six years, as did most of the free world.

Moreover, we have had a disconcerting and distasteful whiff of moralism and institutional self-righteousness in these hearings. Too little have these committees acknowledged that the Executive may well have had a clearer vision of what was at stake in Central America. Too little have we acknowledged that our own convolutions have made the task of the Executive even more difficult. Too little have we confessed that there is real reason to be concerned about the Sieve on Jenkins Hill—the unending leaks which everyone on these committees know exist, and few are willing to take steps to address effectively. That the Executive is a major source of leaked information is a sad truth, but in no way diminishes our own responsibility. No one doubts that the Executive has done some very stupid things in this affair. But one would have liked to have seen some modest acknowledgment of Congressional reponsibility for our present policy impasse.

In nearly thirteen years of service in the House, it has seemed to me that the Congress is usually more eager to assert authority than to accept responsibility; more ready to criticize rather than to constructively propose; more comfortable in the public relations limelight than in the murkier greyness of the real world, where choices must often be made, not between relative goods but between bad and worse. These are not the characteristics that give one confidence in the Congress as a policy-making instrument for America's inescapable encounter with an often-hostile world.

These unsavory character defects are not endemic to this institution. One cannot walk into the old Senate chamber, and travel back, in the mind's eye, to the days when that chamber was filled with the likes of Webster, Calhoun, Clay, Davis, Benton, Houston, Cass, Seward, Chase, and Douglas, and think that the United States Congress cannot do better than it has done in matters of foreign policy over the past ten years. The question is not institutional; it is, in the deepest sense, personal. It has to do with the quality of mind and spirit we bring to our deliberations. It has to do with whether we are playing to the galleries, or to conscience and duty.

We ought to acknowledge that questions of Constitutional propriety have been engaged by these hearings. But we must also acknowledge that there is a deep division in our national legislature over a basic question in world politics. We have, in these hearings, obscured rather than illuminated that division. I bring it to the surface here, not to bait anyone, but in the conviction that only an honest delineation of our differences can lead us beyond posturing to genuine debate. Without that kind of debate, we will continue to flounder in the world, at precisely the historical moment when the tide seems to be shifting in favor of the forces of democracy.

History will not look kindly on us if we miss the opportunities to advance the twin causes of peace and freedom that are before us: in Central America, and throughout the world.

So, as we debate ends and means, let's not obfuscate the deepest ideological and moral issue of our time, which is the contest between freedom and tyranny in the world. To dismiss that contest as the fantasy of an over-heated Cold War mentality is not the act of a morally or politically serious person. Those who see the scalps of General Secord, Robert McFarlane, Admiral Poindexter, and Lt. Col. North as the sure and quick path back to post-Vietnam neo-isolationism are going to reap the whirlwind before this century is out. By all means, let's get our house in order and use means to conduct the great contest in the world that don't corrupt our own democratic processes. But let's not make the argument over means a Trojan

Horse by which neo-isolationism and anti-anticommunism resume dominant positions in our policy debates.

The resurgence of isolationism in our contemporary culture is easily traced.

In the 1970s, several key ideas, developed during Vietnam, came forward in American public life and got lodged in the teaching centers of our culture—the religious leadership, the universities, the prestige press, the popular entertainment industry.

A new form of isolationism arose. It did not teach, as traditional isolationists did, that America should avoid the world because we would be corrupted by it. No, the neo-isolationism of the post-Vietnam era taught that America should stay out of the contest for power in the world because we corrupted the world. What happened when America acted in world affairs? "Vietnam," was the sole answer. No reference to the war against Hitler; no reference to the Marshall Plan and the reconstruction of Japan; no reference to NATO or the Alliance for Progress. No, what happened when America "intervened" in the world was "Vietnam."

And so, paradoxically, the very same people who taught us that the world was "interdependent," also teach us that "intervention" is a very bad thing. This neo-isolationism, as many political commentators have noted over the past decade, has become deeply engrained in the Democratic Party.

We were also taught, in the post-Vietnam period, that anti-communism was culturally passe, historically fallacious, and an inappropriate criterion for guiding U.S. policy. Anti-communism, too, had gotten us "Vietnam." Those who taught this theme were not, in the main, pro-Leninist (as the Old Left was in the 1930's). Rather, they were *anti*-anticommunists. As such, they were willing to give an extraordinary benefit of the doubt to a whole host of Third World communists, each of whom was, in turn, going to get right what Lenin and Stalin had fouled up: Fidel Castro, Ho Chi Minh, Salvador Allende, Maurice Bishop, Mengistu Haile Mariam, the Angolan Eduardo Dos Santos and, finally, Daniel Ortega and the Nicaraguan Sandinistas.

The miserable record of these tyrants speaks for itself, and there is no need to belabor it here. But what we ought to note is how this *anti*-anticommunism was challenged by the people of the Third World. Wherever, in the past decade, people have been given the choice among traditional authoritarianism, a Leninist "new order" and democracy, they have, without exception, chosen democracy. They chose democracy in El Salvador, Honduras and Guatemala. They have chosen democracy in Portugal and Spain. They chose democracy in Argentina and Brazil. They chose democracy in the Philippines. They are trying to build democracy, under great pressure, in the northern provinces of Mexico today. I have no doubt that the great mass of the people of Chile, given the choice, would opt for democracy.

And some people, many of whose leaders had been in the forefront of the revolution against Anastasio Somoza, still wish to choose democracy for Nicaragua. That is what, tragically, our *anti*-anticommunists cannot see.

A third idea let loose by the Vietnam debacle was the notion that military force can never serve the ends of peace, security and freedom. Now those who live in a society of laws should, to be sure, be very careful about the circumstances in which they take up the sword. But in a world persistently hostile to democratic values—a world in which men will starve their opponents to death for political power (as in Ethiopia), or torture them in ways that would defy the imagination of Dante (as in Cuba), or stupefy their minds with drugs (as in the USSR)—it seems odd, at the very least, to assert that the world's principal democratic power should unilaterally reject the use of armed force on all occasions short of the invasion of Long Island.

This teaching was challenged, in a fundamental way, by the successful U.S. action in Grenada—a military intervention for which the people of Grenada expressed overwhelming gratitude. This teaching was being challenged by our support for the Afghan resistance. And this teaching was being challenged by the policy we adopted in the 99th Congress of direct military support for the Nicaraguan democratic resistance. Considerably more was, and is, at stake, than the fate of Daniel Ortega and Adolfo Calero. What was at stake in the Nicaragua debate—and what remains at stake today—is this key teaching in the creed of those who had become accustomed to the high moral ground in the U.S. foreign policy debate since Vietnam—that American military force cannot serve the ends of peace in the world.

Of course, there remain specific questions of legality that have to be clarified. The Courts will wrestle with these questions for years to come, as the Independent Counsel proceeds with his indictments and prosecutions. But, there also are questions of the way in which our foreign policy-making apparently works—or doesn't work.

Beneath these questions of legality and structure, however, there is an even more fundamental argument being engaged here. *It is the question of America's role in the world, and indeed whether we shall have any.*

As we argue over "intervention" and "interdependence," neo-isolationism is being challenged—sometimes skillfully, sometimes clumsily—by the Reagan Administration. That is an important part of what we are arguing about in this affair. The Administration has forthrightly told the leadership of the communist world that the United States proposes to emerge from the paralysis and self-doubt of the Carter era of "malaise" and to re-enter, vigorously, the war of ideas: the on-going battle for the hearts and minds of men and women all over the world. We have tried to be, again, the party of liberty in the world. This has been disconcerting, to say the least, to those who have been taught for almost a generation that America was not on the side of history. However, adequately or inadequately, the Administration has challenged this genteel form of surrender, and has reasserted the idea that history is of *our* making, if we have the wisdom, will and strength for the task. And that is part of what we're arguing about in this affair.

There is an argument over the appropriate use of military force being engaged here. The Administration has made plain—in Grenada, in Libya, in Angola, in Cambodia, in Lebanon, with the Afghan resistance and the Nicaraguan democratic resistance—that it believes that in certain situations armed force can serve the ends of freedom, justice, security and ultimately, peace. Its exercise of that power has been both skillful and, to be candid, less than skillful. But beneath the specific cases to be argued there is the more fundamental point of whether we as a nation are going to eschew the discriminate and proportionate use of armed force for anything other than direct self-defense.

We ought to admit, frankly, that we are, as a nation, deeply divided at these basic choice points. It is one of the great failures of the Reagan Administration that it has not forced these questions out into the open of our public life so that they could be debated civilly and frankly, rather than surreptitiously. Perhaps the providential paradox of our present situation is that these absolutely fundamental questions have been brought to the surface anyway, chiefly through the testimony of Lt. Cot. Oliver North.

And so, beneath the legal and structural arguments; beneath the policy debate; even beneath the challenge to the post-Vietnam orthodoxy that I have so briefly sketched here—there is an absolutely basic question being engaged in the debate over this affair. And that is the question of America. This is not an argument over anyone's patriotism. But survey research has clearly demonstrated that many of America's most influential opinion-shapers and values-teachers respond negatively to the question, "On balance and considering the alternatives, do you consider American power a force for good in the world?" Note the modesty of the question. And yet many of our most prestigious commentators and analysts, many of our most influential scholars, bishops, and rabbis, answer in the negative.

Their teaching has had a profound, and I think debilitating, effect on our public life and our foreign policy for almost a generation. That teaching has gotten itself lodged, to a degree difficult to imagine, in the Congress of the United States and among members of both parties. It is a teaching of despair: perhaps humane despair, perhaps a despair tinged with a sense of the ironic and the contingent in human affairs, but despair nonetheless.

Others of us reject that counsel of despair. We do not claim to have all the answers when the complexities of policy are engaged. We know full well that mistakes have been made by this

Administration, and some acting in the name of this Administration.

But we also know that these were mistakes made because of a judgment that, on balance and considering the alternatives, American power can be a force for good in the world, and that in the hierarchy of values freedom towers above all others.

June 20, 1987

Welcoming the Stranger: A Bicentennial Reflection

T hank you for honoring me with this invitation. As you know, we're celebrating the 200th anniversary of the Constitutional Convention this summer.

I don't think there are any people in the United States more committed to the principles that truly animated the Founders and Framers than the people in this room.

And thank you for the tremendous work you've done, and will do, so that America becomes again what it was always meant to be: a community of hospitality and mutual responsibility where the dignity of human life under God is constitutionally and legally protected for everyone, regardless of age, race, or physical condition.

That is what the Right to Life movement stands for: we stand in defense of the basic moral insight on which the entire American experiment rests.

And that is something I'd like to think about with you tonight: the tenure of our project, and what this means for our commitment to it.

This is the fifteenth National Right to Life convention. Since we first met, almost 20 million of our children waiting to be born have been destroyed. Did that 20 million include the scientist who might have found a cure for cancer or AIDS, the American Mozart, the next Jackie Robinson or Mark Twain or Emily Dickinson? We will never know. That is one measure of the tragedy of the past fifteen years.

There has also been constitutional wreckage this last decade and a half. Scholars from left, right, and center are virtually unanimous in rejecting *Roe* v. *Wade* as shoddy jurisprudence. Yet in many of the opinion-molding sectors of our society, Mr. Justice Blackmun's decision has given the abortion liberty an absolute status afforded virtually no other activity in our republic.

Moreover, the public debate over the abortion liberty remains deeply misinformed, disinformed, and confused:

—It is persistently said that life before birth is not "really" human life. Yet the entire burden of biological evidence developed since *Roe* v. *Wade* is in precisely the opposite direction.

—It is persistently said that *Roe* v. *Wade* "liberalized" abortion law. But, in fact, as constitutional scholar John T. Noonan, Jr., has argued, *Roe* v. *Wade* didn't liberalize abortion law, it abolished abortion law.

—It is persistently said that *Roe* v. *Wade* was a "liberal" decision against "conservative," indeed "reactionary," opposition. In fact, *Roe* v. *Wade* broke a two hundred year-long pattern in which Americans deliberately enlarged the community of those for whom we accept a common responsibility. Slaves were freed, women enfranchised, the elderly protected by Social Security, and the handicapped given easier access to public and private facilities: all in the name of expanding the community of those who are commonly protected and cared for. Then came *Roe* v. *Wade* which, with the stroke of Mr. Justice Blackmun's pen and the acquiescence of six of his colleagues, abruptly declared an entire class of human beings beyond the pale, beyond the boundaries of our community of common concern. This was no "liberal" decision. *Roe* v. *Wade*, not the Right to Life movement, represents the reactionary forces in our society and culture.

—It is still said that *Roe* v. *Wade* only permits "first trimester abortions." In fact, as we all knew then and as we know from bitter experience now, *Roe* v. *Wade* allows abortions up to the moment of birth. The unborn have been summarily stripped of any legal protection since 1973.

—It is said that, whatever its philosophical deficiencies, *Roe v. Wade* enjoys broad popular support. In fact, virtually every public opinion poll taken since 1973 shows a solid consensus *against* abortions of convenience, against abortion as a means of retroactive contraception.

—It is said that we in the Right to Life movement have been guilty of the logical fallacy of the "slippery slope," in our arguments that *Roe* v. *Wade* created a moral and cultural morass. One shouldn't indulge the slippery slope analogy indiscriminately. But fifteen years after *Roe* v. *Wade*, when there is now open discussion of "harvesting" aborted fetal brain tissue and organs; when the begetting and nurturing of children like Baby M is considered a kind of commercial contract, the closest analogue to which is found in horse-breeding; when doctors and some "medical ethicists" agree that infanticide ought to be an available option if the newborn's "quality of life" seems likely to be "insufficient"—in this situation, it is clear that we are not merely in danger of the slippery slope, we're fast careening downward. We're heading down to a modern form of barbarism for many reasons. But can there be any doubt that the culturally crucial push down the slope was given by *Roe* v. *Wade*? The scandal of our age is organized medicine's leadership in justifying the non-treatment of treatable handicapped new-borns, and this was long before the dispute over Baby Doe regulations allowed infanticide to be classified as "post natal abortion." The movement from birth control to death control—the progression from abortion to infanticide to euthanasia—has happened swiftly and almost imperceptibly. The organized medical profession has not protected human life—it has facilitated its wholesale destruction.

—It is argued that abortion is a private medical procedure, privileged by the confidentiality of the physician/patient relationship. The truth, as Father James Burtchaell puts it in his masterful book, *Rachel Weeping*, is far different: "Abortion . . . serves no one's health, and is no medical matter—unless those words be stretched beyond their ordinary meanings. In perhaps 99 percent of present cases it is medical only in virtue of being performed by a physician. It is no more medical than the implantation of silicone in a hopeful lady's bosom."

—Finally, it is still argued, as in the 1984 presidential campaign, that abortion is a sectarian issue, the "imposition" of "Catholic doctrine" on a "pluralistic society." At this fifteenth National Right to Life convention, may I, as a Catholic, respond to that bit of foolishness by citing a brief honor roll of those theologians and philosophers who have taken up scholarly cudgels against the abortion liberty: Paul Ramsey, Stanley Hauerwas, and Albert Outler among the Methodists; Richard Neuhaus and John Strietelmeier among the Lutherans; Harold Brown among Congregationalists; Baruch Brody, David Bleich, David Novak, and Hadley Arkes among Jews. I am proud to be in their company. So are we all.

Looking at this kind of public climate, in which basic facts remain confused, in which the proponents of the abortion liberty are awarded a privileged status by the prestige press, in which it is impossible to conceive a candidate opposed in principle to *Roe v. Wade* being nominated for president by the Democratic Party—looking at this situation, what can we say we have accomplished in these fifteen years of anguish and frustration?

First, and most importantly, we have kept the issue alive. The abortion liberty is not a settled question in the United States. Even our most bitter opponents recognize that, their unilateral declarations of victory notwithstanding. We are not going away. This issue is not going away. And in a political culture where most issues have a half-life of 48 hours, that is no mean accomplishment.

Second, we have had some modest legislative success. Thank you for the important and consistent support you have given the Hyde amendments. Without you, we could not have succeeded in keeping the abortion libertarians' hands out of the Federal treasury. And without these amendments, the Federal treasury would be treating abortion as the moral equivalent of a tonsillectomy. We have now pending in the House of Representatives H.R. 1729 (with a companion bill in the Senate sponsored by Senator Gordon Humphrey R-NH and others.) This bill will permanently prohibit federal funding of abortions, with the "life of the mother" exception, and also forbid the use of Title X family planning funds to any organization that performs or provides referrals for abortion. This bill was initiated by President Reagan, and it now has 106 cosponsors in the House. Our goal is 218 cosponsors, and I hope you'll urge your Congressman and Senators to join us in this historic effort.

Third, we have made converts. Who would have thought, fifteen years ago, that one of our most powerful spokesmen today would be Dr. Bernard Nathanson? Who will be the Bernard Nathanson of the 1990s? There will be one, you may rest assured. Please God, there will be dozens.

But beyond the conversion of major public figures, there are the individual lives you have touched. Yes, almost 20 million of our pre-born children have been destroyed. But how many have been saved because of your individual efforts and your corporate witness? There is some satisfaction, tinged, however, with bitterness and sorrow, in this.

Fourth, there is the size of our movement. Never forget that we are not playing to the galleries. We are witnesses to the truth. We are playing to the angels, and to Him who made the angels. If this movement was reduced, as another movement once was, to a dozen frightened people in a dark room, the cause would still be right, and the cause would go on. The truth of what we do is not measured by the numbers we gather on these and other occasions.

But our persistence and our size—dare I say, our growth?—do mean something important: they mean that America has not become tone deaf to the song we have been singing these past fifteen years. Ours is not a society impervious to the moral cause we are urging. There are ears to hear, and some of them are even hearing. It means something that our call to conscience is heard. It means that the United States has not become indifferent to human suffering. It means that enough of us care. And from that caring, we take hope.

But our hope is not in immediate victory. Were the Court to reverse *Roe* v. *Wade* tomorrow and return us to the *status quo ante* 1973, the argument we press would by no means be settled. We would have fifty arguments on our hands. Some of those we might well win, and quickly. Others would be far more difficult. We are going to have to work on these questions in and out of season. And so, with or without the abortion liberty as defined by *Roe v. Wade*, we are in for a long haul of it. What themes should we be urging in the next years, as the argument continues, and the cause remains so very urgent?

We should, in the first place, learn from international politics: we should practice *linkage*. By that I mean that the question of the right to life is the central thread in a larger tapestry. (Note well please—I did not say "seamless garment"!) That larger tapestry is the American experiment. America has never been simply a mechanical set of arrangements for governance. America, as the great John Courtney Murray taught, is an experiment. And this American experiment is more than an experiment in self-government. It is an experiment in public virtue.

The most important question we face at this bicentennial of the Constitution is not whether we are functionally able to govern ourselves (and believe me, after several months on the Iran-Nicaragua committee, I can tell you that's an open and serious question.) No, the most basic issue is whether we are building the community of character and virtue necessary to support *any* effort at self-government. In a kingdom, it can be enough that the king is virtuous. In a democratic republic, virtuous citizens gathered into a community of character are essential.

In the context of our care and concern for the right to life, this question of public virtue and the building of a community of character involves the moral issue of hospitality.

Hospitality to the stranger is a basic theme in Jewish and Christian ethics. In the Jewish Scripture, Abraham's hospitality to strangers is part of the miraculous process by which the great and surprising gift of his son, Isaac, is given. In the Christian Scripture, in the Gospel of St. Luke, the hospitality to the stranger shown by two downcast disciples talking on the road to Emmaus after the crucifixion of Jesus is the occasion by which the disciples discover the miracle that God has worked in the risen Lord. The Rule of St. Benedict, the foundation of Western monasticism, enjoins the monks to "welcome the stranger as you would welcome Christ."

In our American context, and in the context of this convention, hospitality as a key public virtue is—or should be—a central issue. The public virtue of hospitality has been grievously violated by the abortion liberty. Americans have traditionally been a welcoming people. Virtually everyone in this room is here because his or her parents, grandparents, or great-grandparents were welcomed to these shores as to a new home of freedom and opportunity. Think back on last summer's rededication of the Statue of Liberty, and the words of Emma Lazarus that we heard so often: "Give me your tired, your poor, your huddled masses yearning to breathe free, the wretched refuse of your teeming shore. Send these, the lonely, tempest-tossed to me. I lift my lamp beside the golden door."

Some would call this hokum. I would call it a far more accurate portrait of the American experience, and a far more truthful definition of the American experiment, than the cold, inhospitable, and unwelcoming jurisprudence of Mr. Justice Blackmun and *Roe* v. *Wade*. We have been a hospitable people. We are today, as tens of thousands of refugees will remind us. We could be a hospitable and welcoming society tomorrow, in a more inclusive way, were we to recognize that the abortion liberty in *Roe* v. *Wade* violates our traditions of hospitality.

Stanley Hauerwas of Duke University, a stalwart defender of the right to life and one of America's most eminent moral theologians, has written eloquently of this virtue of hospitality, of its meaning for our cause, and of its implications for building a community of character in America. He speaks of Christians, but his words are true for all of those gathered in this convention:

"Christians are . . . trained to be the kind of people who are ready to receive and welcome children in the world . . . The Christian prohibition of abortion is but the negative side of their positive commitment to welcome new life into their community . . .

"It is, of course, true that children will often be conceived and born under less than ideal conditions, but the church lives as a community which assumes that we live in an age which is always dangerous. That we live in such a time is all the more reason we must be the kind of community that can receive children into our midst. Just as we need to be virtuous, not because virtue pays, but because we cannot afford to be without virtue where it does not pay; so must we be people open to new life. . . From the world's perspective, the birth of a child represents but another drain on our material and psychological resources: children, after all, take up much of the energy that we could use in making the world a better place and our society a more just one. But from the Christian perspective, the birth of a child represents nothing less than our commitment that God will not have this world 'bettered' through the destruction of life." And, may I add, every little baby is not just a tiny new mouth—it is a new pair of hands too.

The American heritage of hospitality is one reflection of the moral claim that undergirds this experiment in freedom: Jefferson's claim, put with clarion simplicity in the Declaration of Independence, that "all men are created equal." In the long view of human history, that claim and the hospitality that flows from it are the exceptions, not the norms. In the long view of history, America is just that: an experiment against the grain.

There is nothing guaranteed about the American proposition. Abraham Lincoln described the Civil War as a great test to determine whether a nation "so conceived and so dedicated" could "long endure." But the testing, Lincoln knew, did not end at Appomattox Court House. Every American generation must respond to that test. That is what self-government in a community of public virtue means: a constant, never-ending test of our character as a people and a civilization.

In this sense, every American is a Founder; every American is a framer. We can look back, as we should, with deep gratitude to the fifty-five remarkable men gathered in a steamy Philadelphia room in 1787. We can marvel at the ingenuity and wisdom with which they devised the world's longest-standing instrument of governance—and free governance, at that.

But the bicentennial of the Constitution is a moment to look ahead as well as to look back. Hindsight can provide insight and foresight. And we need foresight and wisdom and compassion and a reclamation of the tradition of hospitality as we continue the American experiment those brave men launched.

There are many grave threats to our beloved America. We live in a world bitterly divided between the forces of liberty and the forces of a deadly modern tyranny. We live in a world that has become a global political arena—a world in which what happens on the tiny island of Vanuatu in the far Pacific can ultimately make a difference to the future of my home in Bensenville, Illinois. In such a world America has grave responsibilities for protecting and enhancing liberty in the world.

All of these external threats and dilemmas are real. But there are also internal threats to the future of the American experiment. These threats have to do with who we are, not with what we have.

If democracy and the future of this home of freedom demand a virtuous citizenry; if our democratic experiment is an ongoing test of public virtue and our capacity to build a community of character; and if the boundaries of our public hospitality are one index of our public virtue and our character, then the abortion liberty—this terrible shredding of the fabric of our hospitality, this deliberate fracturing of the community of the commonly protected—must be reversed if America is to endure and prosper.

What we are doing now, as a society, is deeply unworthy of us. It is unworthy of our heritage of hospitality to the weak, the poor, the stranger in our midst. It is unworthy of men and women committed to Jefferson's proposition. At the most profound level of our national experience, we are demeaning ourselves as a democratic people.

And so we must do better, and we must do differently. We must reclaim the heritage of public hospitality. We must become again a people capable of welcoming new life, weak life, dependent life, into our midst—*and cherishing it*. We must stop destroying our children waiting to be born. But we shall only stop when we have rediscovered that heritage of hospitality for ourselves.

This is not a task measured in months or even years. It is ongoing. It will continue after *Roe* v. *Wade* becomes a tragic curiosity in our legal textbooks—and that day, my friends, will come. The task we have taken on—this renewing of the American experiment by rediscovering the heritage of hospitality—demands people, leaders, who have assumed responsibility for the long haul, and who can do that because they know what is most urgent in the present moment. That is who you are. Isn't it remarkable that God wanted you to be born at this time and in this place? Not St. Francis of Assisi, not St. Catherine of Siena, not St. Ignatius Loyola—but you?

And He has paid us the terrible compliment of taking us seriously—so what we do is important!

The problem of "theodicy"—Why does God let the world go on the way it is, with all this pain and suffering and evil and anguish?—has bothered sensitive spirits throughout the ages. The Jewish tradition, which knows much about suffering, often addresses the quandary of God and evil through a story, rather than a doctrine. At any moment in history, according to the classic story, the world is preserved because of the actions of 36 just men. Their goodness preserves the world. But they do not know that this is the task which the Lord has given them.

The Jewish story of the just men who preserve the world is a metaphor, I believe, for our movement. The issue here isn't the preservation of the world, but the possibility of American democracy in a situation in which the unborn have been stripped of legal protection. How does the experiment go on? It cannot go on forever amidst this cruel inhospitality. But one reason it has a chance, just now, is because of the just men and women of the Right to Life movement. We know that we have been given a task. We know that we cannot, and will not, lay it down. What we may not realize, and what we must know in this season of the Constitution's bicentennial, is how much the future of the American experiment rests with us. And so, as Sam Levenson has told us, we must believe that each newborn child arrives on earth with a message to deliver to mankind. Clenched in his little fist is some particle of yet unrevealed truth—some missing clue which may solve the enigma of man's destiny. He has a limited amount of time to fulfill his mission and he will never get a second chance—nor will we.

He may be our last hope.

He must be treated as top-sacred.

And so, we are the party of true freedom, which, as Lord Acton taught, is not a matter of doing what you like, but of having the right to do what you ought.

We are the heralds of the classic American claim that "all men are created equal."

We are the men and women of hospitality, the community of welcoming.

And we must be the teachers, in the American third century, of freedom and equality and hospitality. We must help build a community of character, a community that welcomes children and cherishes them. In other words, we must choose Christ or Barabbas!

Depending on that choice, lives will be saved, our republic strengthened, and perhaps—just perhaps at the summing up we will hear the sublime invitation—"Come Beloved of My Father, and enter the Kingdom."

March 20, 1997

Remarks on 'Partial-Birth' Abortion

When you have a theme as large and profound as ours is today, you need the help of great literature to describe the magnitude of the horror of partial-birth abortion. I suppose Edgar Allen Poe could have dealt with it, but it is startling how the words of the ghost of Hamlet's father seem to anticipate our debate today:

> *I could a tale unfold whose lightest word*
> *Would harrow up thy soul, freeze thy young blood,*
> *Make thy two eyes, like stars, start from their spheres,*
> *Thy knotted and combined locks to part,*
> *And each particular hair to stand on end,*
> *Like quills upon the fretful porcupine.*

There is no Member of this House who does not know, in excruciating detail, what is done to a human being in a partial-birth abortion. A living human creature is brought to the threshold of birth. It is four-fifths born. Its tiny arms and legs squirm and struggle to survive. Then its skull is punctured, and the wound deliberately widened; its brains are sucked out; the remains of the deceased are extracted. In the words of the abortion lobby, the baby "undergoes demise."

Something was "rotten in the state of Denmark" in Shakespeare's great drama. Something is rotten in the United States when this barbarity is not only legally sanctioned but declared a fundamental constitutional right. And while we are on Hamlet, who can forget the most famous question in all literature: "To be or not to be"? Every abortion asks that question, but forbids an answer from the defenseless victim.

When this issue was debated in the last Congress, the President and other defenders of partial-birth abortion claimed that the procedure was, in the President's now-familiar euphemism, "rare," and that it was used only in times of grave medical necessity. All of us now know—as many of us knew then—that those claims were lies. Not errors. They were lies! The executive director of the National Coalition of Abortion Providers, Mr. Ron Fitzsimmons, admitted on national television that he and others in the pro-abortion camp simply, flat-out lied about the incidence of partial-birth abortion.

And that was not the only untruth about the procedure. There was the lie that the baby being exterminated feels no pain. That was so far-fetched a lie, so contrary to observable physiological reality, that it was soon supplanted with the argument that anesthesia administered to the mother filters through her system and lets the baby die painlessly. This falsehood outraged an entire profession—anesthesiologists, who denounced it for fear that pregnant women would routinely avoid anesthesia during any medical treatment rather than imperil their unborn child.

Another lie concerned the mother's health. We were told that partial-birth abortions are done only to protect the mother—and on defective fetuses anyway! No. They're done mostly in the fifth and sixth months to healthy women and healthy fetuses. This from Mr. Fitzsimmons' own mouth. All of which gives the lie to the current attempt, in the form of the Hoyer-Greenwood amendment, to gut this bill. It ignores fifth and sixth month partial-birth abortions; and its health exception, understanding court rulings, would allow any woman who claims to be even depressed to get a partial-birth "termination."

As for the case of "defective" fetuses—which is to say, "defective" human beings—there is a family in Oak Park, Illinois, which faced such a tragic situation. When Mrs. Jeannine Wallace French was five months pregnant, her doctor notified her and her husband that one of the twins she was carrying, a daughter named Mary, suffered from a severe neural tube defect. This unborn twin's extreme abnormality complicated the twin pregnancy, and specialists encouraged amniocentesis and abortion. But the French family knew that Mary, though severely disabled, was a member of their family and they protected her from harm. When it became clear that Mary, whose brain had developed outside of her skull, would not survive normal childbirth, a Caesarian delivery was performed.

Born on December 13, 1993, a minute after her healthy big brother Will, Mary lived for six hours cradled peacefully in her father's arms. Baby Mary also gave a special gift to other children—the gift of life. On the day of her funeral, the French family learned that their daughter's heart valves were a match for two Chicago infants, critically ill at the time of Mary's birth. Even babies with medical problems like Mary's can give life or sight or strength to others.

Living less than a day, Mary saved the lives of two other children—because her family ensured that she was granted the dignity which all of us desire, both in life and in death. As parents, we can't protect our children from all pain and suffering. But as Members of this House, today, we can stop the inhumane pain, the terrible suffering, and the needless death caused by partial-birth abortions.

I ask my colleagues: At what point do you get angry at being lied to? What does it say about a policy position that must rely on falsehood, misstatements, and outright lies?

It is *not* the case that these abortions are rare. It is *not* the case that this procedure is used only reluctantly, and in extremis. It is *not* the case that this procedure is used only in instances of medical emergency. Partial-birth abortion—infanticide, in plain English—is business as usual in the abortion industry. That is what the executive director of the National Coalition of Abortion Providers has told us.

Is this House prepared to defend the proposition that infanticide is a fundamental constitutional right? Partial-birth abortion is not about saving life. It is about killing, Killing is an old story in the human drama; fratricide scarred the first human family, according to *Genesis*. But the moral prohibition on killing is as old as the temptation to kill. Most of the familiar translations of the Bible render the commandment, "Thou shalt not kill." A more accurate translation of the Hebrew text would read, "Thou shalt not do murder." Which is to say, thou shalt not take life wantonly, for purposes of convenience, or problem-solving, or economic benefit, nor trade a human life for any lesser value.

The commandment in the Decalogue against "doing murder" is not sectarian dogma. Its parallel is found in every moral code in human history. Why? Because it has been understood for millennia that the prohibition against wanton killing is the foundation of civilization. There can be no civilized life in a society that sanctions wanton killing. There can be no civil society when the law makes expendable the weak and the defenseless and the inconvenient. There can be no real democracy if the law denies the sanctity of every human life.

The Founders of our Republic knew this. That is why they pledged their lives, fortunes, and sacred honor to the proposition that every human being has an inviolable right to life. Our Constitution promises equal protection under the law; our daily pledge is for liberty and justice for all. But where is the protection, where is the justice in partial-birth abortion?

Over more than two centuries of our national history, we Americans have been a people who have struggled to widen the circle of those for whom we acknowledge a common responsibility. Slaves were freed, women were enfranchised, civil rights and voting rights acts passed, our public spaces made accessible to the handicapped, social security mandated for the elderly—all in the name of widening the circle of inclusion and protection.

This great trajectory in our national experience—that of inclusion—has been shattered by *Roe* v. *Wade* and its progeny. By denying an entire class of human beings the protection of the laws, we have betrayed the best in our tradition. We have also put at risk

every life which someone, someday, somehow, might find inconvenient. "No man is an island,'" preached the dean of St. Paul's in
Elizabethan times. He also wrote, "Every man's death diminishes
me, for I am involved in mankind."

We cannot, today, repair all the damage done to the fabric of our
culture by *Roe* and its aftermath. We cannot undo the injustice that
has been done to 35 million tiny members of the human family who
have been summarily killed since the Supreme Court strip-mined
the Constitution to discover therein a fundamental right to abort.
But we can stop the barbarity of partial-birth abortion. We can stop
it, we must stop it, and we diminish our own humanity if we fail.

Historians say that we live in the bloodiest century of human
history: Lenin, Stalin, Hitler, Mao, Pol Pot—the mountains of
corpses reaches to the heavens, and hundreds of millions cry out for
justice. We cannot undo the horrors inflicted on the human spirit.
We cannot heal the wounds already sustained by civilization. We
can only say, "Never again."

But in saying "Never again," we commit ourselves to defend
the sanctity of life. In saying "No" to the horrors of twentieth century slaughter, we solemnly pledge not to "do murder"—because
honoring that pledge is all that stands between us and the moral
jungle.

Mr. Speaker, distinguished colleagues of the Congress, we have
had enough of the killing. The constitutional fabric of our government and our society has been shredded by an unenumerated abortion license, which thus far has included the vicious cruelty of partial-birth abortion. The moral culture of our country is eroding
when we tolerate a cruelty so great that its proponents do not even
wish us to learn the facts about this "procedure."

The Congress has been blatantly, willfully, maliciously lied to
by proponents of the abortion license. Enough. Enough of the lies.
Enough of the cruelty. Enough of the distortion of the Constitution.
There is no constitutional right to commit this barbarity.

That is what I ask you to affirm. In the name of humanity let us
do so, for in the words of Saint Paul, "NOW is the acceptable
time"!

September 19, 1996

"An Unspeakable Horror"—Debate on the Clinton Veto

In the classic Russian Novel, *Crime and Punishment*, Dostoyevsky has his murderous protagonist Raskolnikov complain that "Man can get used to anything, the beast!" The fact that we are even debating this issue—that we have to argue about the legality of an abortionist's plunging a pair of scissors into the back of the neck of a child whose trunk, arms, and legs have already been born, and then suctioning out his brains—only confirms Dostoyevsky's harsh truth. We were told in the Judiciary Committee by a nurse in attendance during a partial-birth abortion that the little arms and legs stop flailing and suddenly stiffen as the scissors is plunged in. The people who like to say, "I feel your pain," can't be referring to that little infant.

What kind of people have we become that this "procedure" is even a matter for discussion? Can't we draw the line at torture? And if we can't, what has become of us? We are incensed at ethnic cleansing in the Balkans. How then can we tolerate infant cleansing here at home?

There is no argument here about when a human life begins. The child who is destroyed is unmistakably alive, unmistakably human, and unmistakably brutally killed.

I have finally figured out why supporters of abortion on demand fight this infanticide ban tooth and claw. It is because, for the first time since *Roe* v. *Wade*, the focus of the debate is squarely on the baby and the harm that abortion inflicts on the unborn child—or, in this case, a child who is four-fifths born. That child, whom the advocates of abortion have done everything in their power to dehumanize, is as much the bearer of human rights as any Member of this House. To deny those rights is more than the betrayal of a powerless individual whom some find burdensome. It is to betray the central promise of America: that there is, in this land, justice for all. That is why advocates of abortion on demand, having detached themselves from any sympathy for the unborn child, have also separated themselves from the instinct for justice that gave birth to our country.

President Clinton, reacting angrily to the Congress' challenge to his veto of the partial-birth ban, claimed not to understand the morality of our position. He asserts a morality of "compassion" for those who engage in a practice which Senator Moynihan called indistinguishable from infanticide. Not that it will really matter to Mr. Clinton, let me explain that there is no moral or medical justification for this barbaric assault on a partially born infant. Dr. Pamela Smith, Director of Medical Education in the Department of Obstetrics and Gynecology at Chicago's Mt. Sinai Hospital, testified to that.

Quite a different "doctor," the abortionist who is the principal perpetrator of these atrocities, Martin Haskell, has conceded that at least 80% of the partial-birth abortions he performs are entirely elective, and he admits to over 1,000 of them.

We have been told about some extreme cases of malformed babies, as though life is only for the privileged, the planned, and the perfect. But Dr. James McMahon cited nine such abortions simply because the child had a cleft lip.

Other physicians have made it clear that this procedure is never a medical necessity but merely a "convenience" for those who choose to abort late in pregnancy, when it becomes physically difficult to dismember the unborn child in the womb.

The President's claim that he wants to "solve a problem" by adding a "health" exception to the legislation is spurious. As any-

one who has spent ten minutes studying current federal law understands—and I know that includes Mr. Clinton—any "health"
exceptions are so broadly construed by the courts as to make a ban
meaningless.

There is one consistent commitment that has survived the twists
and turns of policy during this Administration; and that is its
unshakable commitment to a legal regime of abortion on demand.
Nothing is, or will, be done to make abortion "rare." No legislation
or regulatory act will be allowed to impede the most permissive
abortion license in the democratic world. Mr. Clinton would do us
all a favor, and make a modest contribution to the health of the
democratic process, if he would simply concede the obvious and
spare us further exhibitions of his manufactured grief.

In one of his memoirs, Dwight D. Eisenhower, writing about
the death toll in World War II, said, "The loss of lives that might
have otherwise been creatively lived scars the mind of the civilized
world." Mr. Speaker, our souls have been scarred by more than one
million abortions in this country every year. Our souls have so
much scar tissue that there isn't room for any more.

What do we mean by "human dignity" if we subject innocent
children to brutal execution when they are almost delivered? We all
hope and pray for "death with dignity," but what is dignified about
death by scissors stabbed into your neck so your brains can be suc-
tioned out? We have had long and bitter debates in this House about
"assault weapons." Those scissors and that suction machine are
assault weapons worse than any AK-47. You might miss with an
AK-47; the abortionist never misses.

It isn't just the babies who are dying for the lethal sin of being
unwanted. We are dying, not from the darkness, but from the cold:
the coldness of self-brutalization that chills our sensibilities and
allows us to claim this unspeakable act is an act of "compassion."
If you vote to uphold the President's veto, if you vote to maintain
the legality of a "procedure" that is revolting to even the most hardened heart, then please do not use the word "compassion" ever
again.

I am not in the least embarrassed to say that I believe we will one day each be called upon to render an account for what we have done, and what we have failed to do, in our lifetime. And while I believe in a merciful God, I would be terrified at the thought of having to explain, at the final judgment, why I stood unmoved while Herod's slaughter of the innocents was being reenacted here in my own country.

This debate has been about an unspeakable horror. And while the details are graphic and grisly, it has been, I think, helpful for all of us, and for our country, to recognize the full brutality of what goes on in America's abortuaries, day in and day out, week after week, month after month, year after year. We are not talking about abstractions here. We are talking about life and death at their most elemental. And we ought to face the truth of what we oppose, or support, stripped of all euphemisms.

We have talked so much about the grotesque. Permit me a word about beauty. We all have our own images of the beautiful: the face of a loved one, a dawn, a sunset, the evening star. I believe that nothing in this world of wonders is more beautiful than the innocence of a child. Do you know what a child is? He or she is an opportunity for love; and a handicapped child is an even greater opportunity for love.

Mr. Speaker, we risk our souls—we risk our humanity—when we trifle with that innocence, or demean it, or brutalize it. We need more caring and less killing.

Let the innocence of the unborn have the last word in this debate. Let their innocence appeal to what President Lincoln called "the better angels of our nature." Prove Raskolnikov wrong. Declare that partial-birth abortion is something we will never get used to. Make it clear, once again, that there *is* justice for *all*—even the most defenseless in this land.

Summing Up

*Ronald Reagan and HJH, happy warriors in
the battle against Communism and for freedom.*

A t a certain age, one is expected to ramble in one's conversations. In my case, as a practitioner of Chicago's neighborhood politics, it's been a lifelong habit, and I'll take every chance to indulge it. After all, a final chapter, in both the literary sense and otherwise, is only what we make of it, and I do have a few more things to say. There is, however, something rather disconcerting in that finality. It brings to mind a "Peanuts" strip of long ago, in which Charlie Brown laments that he and his pals would not be around to see their newly planted tree at its maturity. "Why," responds Linus, "are we going somewhere?" In today's culture of perpetual youth, perhaps even an octogenarian may be permitted to share Linus' naiveté about the future, which may explain the generally upbeat tone of the three speeches that follow this introduction.

Do not look therein for nuance. I have been known to wear my heart on my sleeve, and in the case of these addresses, I guess it's true. Perhaps it's a generational thing, from a time when people weren't so self-conscious about what they cherished and respected. There was little room for ironic detachment in the world of the Great Depression, World War, and the Holocaust. Today's young adults grew up on the hipness of "Seinfeld," while Americans of my age could be moved by Red Skelton's classic silent portrayal of an old man saluting the passing flag. And yet, whenever I have visited with those youngsters barely one-quarter of my age, I generally find the same decency, the same hopefulness, and so often the same idealism that I long ago found in the young men—kids, some of them—who were my crew in the South Pacific.

Speaking of youth, or rather, to them, the last speech in this volume is a commencement address, variations of which I used at several colleges and universities over the years. From New England to the South to the Midwest, my subject was basically the same: the moral basis of a free society. An old friend of mine has observed that, in post-Christian America, there are only two universally recognized norms for determining whether something is ethically acceptable: Is it deductible? And can it be covered by insurance? (Some would add a third consideration: Is it environmentally sustainable?) I doubt we have gone quite that far in the direction of secularism, though much of our judicial system certainly has. The unexpected resurgence, over the last two decades, of what the Left witlessly calls the "religious Right" has given me renewed hope in the ability of average Americans to assert their values and defend their traditions against those who dominate so much of our public culture.

More than at any other time in my long career, today it seems to me that America is close to unique in the religious underpinning of its political system. I'm referring to the virtually universal belief, in the early days of our Republic, that public virtue is a prerequisite for a republican form of government. That isn't theology; it's just a common-sense extension to the political realm of Samuel Johnson's wariness concerning an individual: "If he really does think that there is no distinction between virtue and vice . . . when he leaves our houses, let us count our spoons." Most Americans today, I think, tend to agree, though they might use other words to express the same idea.

That idea has international implications. As closely tied as we are to our European allies in political outlook, there is in reality a great and widening gulf between us. It is a radical divergence concerning the role of religion, and religious believers, in public affairs. Hence the disdain, or worse, from European elites toward American leaders, like George W. Bush, who publicly profess their faith and openly pray for divine guidance. A European Union which cannot bring itself even to mention, in its fundamental charter, the Christian culture from which it emerged is deracinated, that is, cut off from its roots. Culturally adrift, intellectually defenseless in the face of various "isms," today's Europe faces a withering future; and I cannot see how anything short of a religious awakening, on the order of the great Methodist social renewal in 19th Century

England, can restore its social prospects. Lest anyone on this side of the Atlantic assume that the outcome is none of our business, consider the future of America's world leadership when it is tied in tandem with allies whose fundamental values may pull them in a contrary direction. That is not a happy outlook.

There is, however, considerable reason for optimism about the future of our own representative democracy, and that positive outlook dominates the three speeches which follow this introduction. My optimism does not, however, lie in the strength of our economy or the prowess of our military or, least of all, the overall quality of those whom we elect to office. Two of the factors that give me the greatest encouragement are the democratization of information systems and the growth of consumer control of education. Those two trends are, I believe, our best bets for maintaining a system of ordered liberty for future generations.

Whether or not Marx's famous dictum—that the key to power is controlling the means of production—was ever accurate, it is irrelevant today. In a society like ours—post-industrial, technotronic, in some senses borderless—having the key to the factory is nowhere near as important as having the key to the classroom or to the newsroom.

Let's take education first. Government control of schooling is far more dangerous than government control of the workplace (though I'm emphatically against that too.) Most nations of the world, to the extent that they have school systems, still operate within the context of government-run schools—to the startling extent, for example, that home-schooling is basically illegal in today's Germany, which still operates under a Nazi-era education statute. In the United States, on the other hand, the momentum for the last several decades has been strongly in the opposite direction, toward an unprecedented diversity of educational choices and, hence, toward increasing fragmentation of the power that comes from shaping education.

Some find this disconcerting. The National Education Association, like any other group that profits from a monopoly, accurately considers freedom in schooling a threat to its power.

From a different direction, some neo-conservative intellectuals yearn for the restoration of what they would call a common culture, to ensure that all American youngsters learn the same history, math and language skills. More than a century ago, that was the goal of the founders of public education in this country, and it was reinforced during the Progressive Era with the intent of assimilating the great influx of immigrants from southern and eastern Europe. I can understand why, faced with our current ethnic and linguistic divisions, some would seek to standardize the learning process, as a way of guarding against centrifugal cultural forces. But their reliance on initiatives of the federal government to impose uniformity on learning strikes me as both constitutionally inappropriate and practically impossible.

For conservatives, for libertarians—heck, for any group that wants to maintain its values and pass along its heritage to future generations, all of which is an essential element of liberty—minimizing the role of government in schooling has to be a priority. And the best way to do that is to minimize governmental mandates about education while maximizing choice at all levels of learning. In this country, while we do have very serious problems with federal intrusion into local school systems, we also have greater diversity in educational opportunities than at any time in the past. As long as American families are free to select the best kinds of schooling for their particular needs and aspirations, their children will have a good chance to grow up without the statist indoctrination inherent in a uniform, nationalized system.

The same schema applies to the production and dissemination of information, which, I would argue, has been the single most important change in American life during my entire public career. Today's young staffers on Capitol Hill cannot begin to understand how limited we used to be, in communicating and advocating our policies, when television was dominated by the three major networks, there were no fax machines, no computers, and powerful urban newspapers could sway public opinion with their predictably liberal editorials. Apart from their own few magazines and papers,

Conservatives had to scramble for whatever coverage, or air time, or print space they could wrangle. And it was só often a losing battle against the entrenched liberalism of what might be called the information industry.

The Berlin Wall wasn't the only barrier that collapsed during the Age of Reagan. Most of us, myself included, were unaware that we were being swept by technology—by the human ingenuity behind it, really—into a whole new political ballgame, in which conservatives would no longer have to rely on the grudging beneficence of the media establishment to get our message to the public. The eruption of conservative talk-radio, cable news and other competition for the old networks, the decline of the traditional newspaper business, and, most of all, the universal spread of the Internet have finally given conservatives what had long seemed our impossible dream: equal access to the hearts and minds of the American people.

Of course, it isn't just for us. Most of the world has been going through the same dizzying experience. Within the span of a decade, we moved from the time when Romania's pathologically Communist regime required the registration of typewriters as a means of information control to the time when China's schizophrenically Communist regime attempts to censor the Internet (and often succeeds, with the dishonorable assistance of foreign capitalists as the price of "doing business" in the workers' paradise.) Eventually, I expect information technologies to out-maneuver even China's control mechanisms. By their very nature, those technologies will empower any group that learns to employ them. Hence, the rise of bloggers, responsible and otherwise, and information streams to suit every imaginable opinion (as well as some that are better left unimagined).

On the political side in this country, we are swamped with a veritable tsunami of opinion and information, from Internet to newsletters, from attack ads to drive-by journalism. Much of it will always be unreliable; some of it may be cruel and unfair. But that's not much different from the supposedly objective journalism long practiced by many members of the liberal news elite. Nothing educates one's taste buds as quickly as a dose of one's own medicine. So needless to say, not everyone has been happy with the political consequences of the information revolution. Hence the various proposals to restrict, by one means or another, what citizens can say about candidates, or when they can say it, or how much of their own money they can use to get the message across. In other words, Campaign Reform—because those restrictions on free speech and political participation are what that issue is really all about: the most extensive abridgement of the First Amendment since the Alien and Sedition Acts of 1800.

There are few practices more insidious than claiming to clean up politics by hobbling your opponents and tilting the playing field in your own favor. That, however, is a fair assessment of the various election laws, campaign regulations, and court decisions which disadvantage third-parties, insurgent causes, challenger candidates, and independent issue campaigns, while concentrating power in traditional, centralized party systems. Citizen participation in the political process is a commendable thing, it seems, as long as it is kept within certain bounds. But what good is it to have your choice of any car on the lot if they all turn out to be Edsels?

Most Americans are familiar with the great Norman Rockwell painting, one of his "Four Freedoms" series, portraying, in a glimpse of a New England town meeting, the freedom of speech. Its central figure is a workingman, standing to speak his mind while the other townsfolk listen attentively. His face is weathered and his hands hardened by labor, but he clearly has the respect of his neighbors. No one would dare tell him to shut up and sit down. But just wait until he runs afoul of the latest campaign reform regulations for contributing to an organization that publicized an incumbent's voting record too close to election day! I don't think he would let himself be pushed around that way, nor do I think most of today's Americans will stand for it either. They've already rendered their verdict on the liberals' toe-in-the-door approach to public funding of campaigns; the IRS check-off system is going belly up because of non-participation by the taxpayers. There went the end-game of the campaign reformers.

Keeping in mind the issues we've just explored, it was probably presumptuous for me to entitle one of the following speeches,
"Twenty-First Century Government." Fact is, the most important
changes in society and politics usually develop slowly, over time,
and we do not feel their real impact until it's too late to do much
about them. I recall, for example, a prescient article from the early
1970s, when much was being made of the supposed "greening"—
social and environmental liberalization—of America. The article
asked a different question: Will the "greening" turn blue? Blue as
in, blue collar—and the rise of young men and women from outside
the customary circles of privilege, Ivy League schools, and Wasp
backgrounds. Three decades later, what was something of an unher-
alded proletarian revolution has opened up American politics as
never before. In the process, it has fundamentally changed the
Republican Party. It was, in large part, the rising children of the old
working class—a cadre heavily Catholic and evangelical—who
made possible the Reagan coalition and turned it into a modern
majority.

One anecdote may illustrate the point. During closed-door consideration of the 1980 Republican Platform, a distinguished member of the United States Senate lamented that adding a pro-life position to attract Catholic women would drive Republican women out
of the party. He was reprimanded by a gutsy staffer, just the kind of
person I described above, who had already done a tour of duty at
the White House and wasn't easily intimidated. The Senator—who,
let it be said, was a gentleman and no bigot—apologetically backed
down, but it was already too late for him or anyone else to halt the
demographic transformation of their GOP.

With a political party, as with any living organism, change is a
sign of vitality. One case in point: Most Republican Members of
Congress will tell you that free trade is the "traditional position" of
their party; and they really believe it, unaware that, before the last
few decades, the GOP had been virulently protectionist from its
very beginning. In politics, a long memory can be a liability, as candidates have to adapt their views to changing circumstances at
home and around the world. So it would be foolish to think that fur-

ther transformations are not forthcoming for both major parties; and for Republicans, perhaps, a conservative inclusion of much of the Hispanic community. That prospect is no more unthinkable than today's reality of Catholic and southern support for a party which, a century ago, ran against "rum, Romanism, and rebellion."

In my musings about the future, as in the speeches that follow, I prefer to concentrate on the things which do not, or should not, change. First and foremost, I would place the force of personal commitment. One can exercise enormous power without being in an officially powerful role. Some of the most effective Members of Congress over the years have had their impact from adherence to principle, rather than from a Leadership post or committee chairmanship. Through much of their careers, for example, Chris Smith in the House and Jesse Helms in the Senate were backbenchers, scorned by some, underestimated by many; but their sheer determination won them the grudging admiration of their colleagues and, ultimately, their votes.

The corollary to what I have just said is that positions of power are always temporary, and usually more temporary than those who hold them expect them to be. It's tough enough to climb the heights; but when the tops are reached, the slopes get unexpectedly (and sometimes unjustly) slippery—a lesson learned in bipartisan fashion by Jim Wright, Newt Gingrich, Tony Coelho, Dan Rostenkowski, Tom Delay, and many others. The famous ones come and go; but those who labor for a good cause in the vineyards of politics have reason to keep on keeping on.

The classic example of that is William Wilberforce, the English reformer who, more than any other individual, awoke the conscience of his country to end the slave trade in 1807 and to end slavery itself throughout the Empire in 1833. He was told that glorious news only three days before his death, but he must have long known in his heart that it would one day come, whether or not he would live to hear it. His crusade brings to mind the little plaque Ronald Reagan kept on his presidential desk in the Oval Office, a daily reminder that there's no telling how much you can achieve as long as you don't care who gets the credit. That was true in

Parliament two centuries ago and remains true in American politics today.

Those who aspire to a political career would do well to learn a lesson from the artists of the Renaissance, who would sometimes include themselves in their great religious paintings, but not as central figures. They might place themselves as a face in the crowd or an on-looker at the edge of the canvas. That was enough exposure for them. And so for us. Whenever our cause is noble, whenever the work is glorious, then especially we can be content with a place on the sidelines, knowing we have been part of a mighty enterprise, a good fight. Knowing, indeed, the wisdom of the old protest song, that although one man's hands can't set the world aright, "if two and two and fifty make a million, we'll see that day come 'round."

November 16, 1999

Democracy
and Virtue

O ne hundred and thirty-six years ago, in a little cemetery in
Pennsylvania, one of Illinois' most illustrious sons asked a
haunting question: Whether a nation conceived in liberty,
and dedicated to the proposition that all men are created equal, can
long endure. Since that day at Gettysburg, each succeeding generation of Americans has had to answer that question for themselves,
For our generation the answer to that question is by no means certain, as we find ourselves deeply troubled today by questions of
trust and honesty—indeed, by the question of whether those qualities still have any meaning in our public life.

When one thinks of Honor, the signers of the Declaration of
Independence, America's birth certificate, come to mind. One of the
many remarkable things about their Declaration is that it acknowl-
edges that political authority—which is to say, political
legitimacy—comes directly from the Creator to the people, who
then lend it to the State. In Europe at the time, it was the other way
around. Power went from the Creator to the State, in the person of
the monarch, which might then parcel it out to one or another portion of the people.

But the Founders of this country had a different political theology, and to it they were willing to sacrifice their all. There is a monument at Berkeley plantation on the James River in Virginia that
reminds us: "By signing the Declaration of Independence the 56
Americans pledged their lives, their fortunes, and their sacred
honor. It was no idle pledge—nine signers died of wounds during

the Revolutionary War; five were captured or imprisoned; wives and children were killed, jailed, mistreated, or left penniless; twelve signers' houses were burned to the ground; seventeen lost everything they owned. No signer defected—their honor, like their nation, remained intact."

Today, we Americans must ask whether Honor can become sacred again, rather than quaint. Consider where we are at the end of the Twentieth Century. Over 223 yeas of independence, the United States has survived constitutional crises, civil war, horrendous epidemics, a great depression, several economic crashes, two world wars, a host of smaller conflicts, and the long, hard "peace" of the Cold War. And the nation has survived it all!

We are the world's only super-power. We enjoy a level of material prosperity unprecedented in history. In these happy circumstances, do we really have to worry about the state of our politics? Or whether there is a moral basis of rectitude and honor sufficient to sustain a free society?

I believe we do. And we have to be concerned not only about the perennial dangers of sleaze and corruption, venality and the coarsening of public life. Some things come along with human nature and are always with us. But today a different kind of danger threatens our democracy. That danger is cynicism—the widespread notion that all of politics is corrupt and sleazy and venal, and that all politicians are, by definition, corrupt, sleazy and venal.

That cynicism among the American people is an acid eating away at the vital organs of our public life. It is a real and present danger. It is the worst of all corruptions in any democracy. Why? Because cynicism about politics blinds us to the fact that each one of us is responsible for the common good of our community, our state, and our country. Cynicism blinds us to the nobility of being a self-governing people. Cynicism makes us forget the continuing truth of what Abraham Lincoln said of these United States: that this democracy is the last best hope of man on earth.

A cynical people cannot, over time, sustain a democracy. Democracy rests on an act of faith, in fact, millions of them, professed by citizens one by one. Cynicism corrodes faith.

If we want to hand our children and grandchildren and great-grandchildren the American democracy for which many of us have risked our lives, we must confront, then challenge, then reverse the cynicism that is pervasive in our public life today. We need once again, as some previous generations have needed, what Lincoln called a "new birth of freedom," generated by faith, hope, and a commitment to the common good.

Democracy is about self-governance, rule "of the people, by the people, and for the people," to use the simple eloquence from that day at Gettysburg. But what kind of people can be self-governing? We know that, over the long run of history, democracy has been the exception, not the rule. Happily, today, in many parts of the world, democracy is on the march; for liberty is an aspiration that animates peoples all over the earth. But even while we rejoice in the widespread conviction of democracy's superiority to other forms of government, we must take care to understand that democracy is not something that simply happens. Nor is it merely a matter of the mechanics of popular government: free elections, an independent judiciary, constitutionally protected civil and religious rights, and rules for how we sue one another.

Democracy is, at the bottom line, a matter of people. As our own Founders, those men commemorated on that memorial in Virginia, knew well, only a certain kind of people can be self-governing for any length of time. Those who wish to be self-governing in their public affairs must first govern themselves from within, by a moral code that teaches them the virtues necessary for the survival of free institutions.

It's actually very simple: You cannot have a self-governing country without self-governing citizens. You cannot have a system that guarantees liberty and justice for all unless you have a people capable of living out their freedom in such a way that it brings forth justice. In sum, democracy requires a virtuous people.

So if we seek a new birth of freedom in the Twenty-first Century, it will have to come from a rebirth of virtue among us. From that rebirth of virtue—or morality, or character, or whatever other name we apply—can come the remoralization of our politics.

Part of that process must be the election of public officials who can cut through the fog of cynicism that is choking our politics: men and women who earn the respect of those who elect them—and who can retain that respect once they are in office.

One more word—or caution—about freedom. It is a public good, not merely a private privilege. Certain current justices of the U.S. Supreme Court seem to believe in a free-floating right of personal autonomy that sounds more like a teenager's dream world than a sane jurisprudence. Our Founders believed that God made us free so that we could freely seek the good, the noble, the just, and the true. In other words, wielding our liberty, we could build a decent society. And so we did, in general, eventually trying to correct some terrible mistakes, like slavery and the treatment of Native Americans. But all that we have achieved over two centuries and more has been done within the concept of a single national identity. The pundit Charles Krauthammer has called this "our great national achievement, fashioning a common citizenship and identity for a multi-ethnic, multi-lingual, multi-racial people," and he's right. That common identity, which may be unique in the human experience, is the social context within which we individual Americans exercise our liberty.

We can only wonder how our liberty is to be exercised if we lose that unifying context of national identity. That is a very real prospect as we contemplate the future of our body politic. Almost every facet of contemporary society—schools, the arts, even the law—now encourages division by race, ethnicity and gender. This deliberate Balkanization not only runs counter to our best traditions; it threatens to replace the idea of individual rights with the alien notion of group entitlement.

All of which is to say that, for proponents of ordered liberty, for advocates of responsible freedom, for devotees of constitutional government, for defenders of the Bill of Rights, there is much work ahead, and great labors to be undertaken, so that we can someday say, as earlier generations could say: We have preserved this Republic. We have renewed its moral foundations. We have kept it united, and we bequeath to the future its priceless liberties.

November, 1999

Twenty-First Century Government

The 21st century will be the third century of modern democracy. If the 19th century was modern democracy's infancy, and the 20th its adolescence, can we expect that the 21st century will be the century of modern democracy's first maturity?

Historical statisticians tell us that democratic self-government has been something of an anomaly in recorded history. Most men and women, during the past 3,500 years, have been ruled by authoritarianisms of one sort or another. The habit of authoritarianism dies hard; in the third decade of our own 20th century, reasonable men and women, some of them distinguished intellectuals, were arguing that the authoritarianism of fascism was the only way to cope with explosive social and economic turbulence of modern society. They were wrong. But their example should be a warning signal to us.

We can also take heart from the fact that democracy is not thought to be an anomaly by billions of men and women around the world today; rather they think of democratic self-government as a basic human right.

This widespread conviction that freedom is not simply the expedient thing, but the right thing, is one of the most important of public facts on the threshold of a new century and a new millennium. At the end of a century of tears, there is a new hope in the world.

That hope will be vindicated if democratic self-government continues to prove itself capable of sustaining free and just societies in the 21st century.

Which brings us to the question I want to address: "what kind of government in the 21st century?"

I'm from Illinois, so in thinking about such large questions, I instinctively turn to Abraham Lincoln, the greatest son of my state and surely one of the greatest of Americans. In his epic Gettysburg Address, President Lincoln defined democracy as government "of the people, by the people, and for the people." Those three prepositions—"of", "by", and "for"—give us some clues to the "kind of government" required if the 21st century is to vindicate the world's great hope for democracy.

To speak of democracy as government "of the people" requires us to think about the kind of people who can make democracy work. It requires us to think about the *character* of a democratic people.

Democracy is not a machine that will run of itself. Democratic self-government requires a people who are capable of being self-governing; people who have made their own certain moral and political values. Chief among those values are honesty and tolerance.

"Honesty" and "tolerance" may seem to be values in tension. In fact, they are mutually reinforcing and complementary.

Honest debate is the lifeblood of democracy. Without honesty in the public discourse—without a broad public understanding, shared by public officials, that lying has no place in the democratic public square—democracy withers and dies. A monarchy or tyranny can survive mendacity. A democracy cannot.

Tolerance is not the opposite of honesty, but its complement. Tolerance, rightly understood, is not toleration of dishonesty or the hedging of differences; tolerance is the forthright, honest *engagement* of differences, within the bond of democratic civility. A free society is, by its very nature, disputatious. The virtue of tolerance—the moral habit of dealing with differences openly, honestly, and respectfully—is what allows a democratic people to work through their disputes with the kind of decency that strengthens civil society and the democratic political process.

So the first lesson to be drawn from Lincoln's definition of democracy for the government of the 21st century is that the vindication of democracy demands an honest, tolerant citizenry, and honest, tolerant public officials—a citizenry and its representatives capable of building agreement across divisions because arguments are honestly engaged.

Then there is government "*by* the people."

Some political theorists may speculate about the return of "direct" or plebiscitary democracy through the computer revolution. But it seems to me that the "kind of government" we can—and ought to—expect in the 21st century will be *representative* democracy, in which the people choose representatives to decide issues of the common good. This immediately raises the question of the kind of people capable of serving as the people's representatives.

In democracy's infancy and its adolescence, there were heated debates about qualifications for public office. Should only property-owners be allowed to vote and to serve in public office? What about women? What about those of a different race, or religion, or ethnic origin than the majority?

Those questions have largely been settled, as we stand on the threshold of what should be democracy's first period of maturity. Men and women, blacks, whites, Asians, Hispanics, Protestants, Catholics, Jews, Muslims, atheists and agnostics: all, in American democracy, are welcome in the public square, and all can propose themselves as the people's representatives. Race, creed, sex, and ethnicity, we have come to understand, cannot be qualifiers or disqualifiers, if ours is to be a government truly "*by* the people."

But that leaves a large question unsettled: the question of the moral qualifications of the people's representatives.

Public office is a public trust: thus the first moral qualification for public office is trustworthiness.

Public office is a matter of making judgments about the common good; thus the second moral qualification for public office is the virtue of prudence.

Public office involves debate—often heated—about what constitutes the common good; thus the third moral qualification for public office is tolerance, of the kind I described a moment ago— the virtue of being able to disagree agreeably, civilly, tolerantly.

Public office is a privilege; thus the fourth qualification for public office is the willingness to sacrifice personal gain for the common good. As I once told a group of newly-elected Members of Congress, if they did not know what they were prepared to lose office for, they were going to do a lot of damage during their congressional careers.

Government "*by* the people" involves a compact of trust between the people and their representatives. When that compact is broken—by a lack of trustworthiness, by imprudence, by intolerance, by self-serving—democracy suffers in consequence.

Finally, there is government "*for* the people."

The good to be served by government is the public's good, the common good, not the private goods of selfish individuals. At the end of democracy's 20th century adolescence, we hear voices suggesting that the pursuit of the common good is really just a matter of democratic *procedures*—that government "*for* the people" does not involve certain basic moral judgments. This, I think, is a seriously mistaken notion.

Democratic self-government rests on a foundation of moral consensus. The most secure foundations of government "of the people, by the people, and for the people" are not what James Madison called the "parchment barriers" of constitutions and treaties, but the habits—the *virtues*—of a people. Absent those virtues, democracy is imperiled.

Democracy of the kind we should want to flourish in the 21st century cannot be simply a matter of the political and legal procedures by which we agree to settle our differences. If you and I disagree, and if neither of us recognizes a moral standard beyond us by which we can adjudicate our differences, then the only way to settle the argument between us is for one of us to impose his will over the other. If tens of millions of people are on one side of an issue, and tens of millions on the other, and neither side recognizes a moral standard by which to settle the disagreement without violence, then violence is almost certain to ensue.

That is why we must, on the threshold of the century of democracy's maturity, rebuild some of the moral foundations of democracy.

We must be able to say again, publicly, why the human person enjoys certain inalienable rights, most especially including the right to life, simply because he or she is a human being.

We must be able to say again, publicly, why democracy is a superior form of government to tyranny or anarchy.

We must be able to give an account—a *moral* account—of our conviction that democratic civility and tolerance are truly *goods*, not simply conveniences.

In a word: government *"for* the people" in the 21st century will require us to think again about the nature of freedom, as freedom *for* the truth about human beings, their inherent nobility, and their inalienable dignity.

In the years since the collapse of Communism, we have heard a fair amount about the defects of western democracy and the superiority of alternative forms of government. There is a deafening silence about such claims from East Asia these days, and with good reason: benign, paternalistic authoritarianism has shown itself incapable of sustaining prosperous societies.

To note this is not to suggest that western democracies are defect-free: on the contrary, I believe, as I have just suggested, that western democracies in general, and the United States in particular, have an enormous task of moral and cultural reconstruction to do if the 21st century is to vindicate the hopes vested in democracy in the century now drawing to a close.

But I remain convinced that freedom—as a method for discerning and adhering to the truth—is what the creator built into human beings.

And that is why, for all its present difficulties, I am hopeful about democracy's future, and the future of government "of, by, and for the people," in the 21st century.

As we look into a new century and a new millennium, we can see science and technology opening up horizons of possibility that were once beyond human imagination.

The biological revolution that has broken open the secrets of the gene may well have an impact on human affairs as profound as the revolution in physics that broke open the secrets of the atom.

The atomic revolution in physics made possible cheap electricity and propulsion; it also handed humanity the keys to self-destruction. The new bio-technology revolution promises us once-inconceivable conquests over illness, age, and the fear that have accompanied them in millennia. It, too, has a shadow side: it tempts us to manipulate our species and our future.

This is neither the time nor the place to explore this complex and fascinating set of issues. Let me say only this. In the 21st century, a century of great possibility and equivalent danger, the character of the American people will be tested as never before.

Washington is a city that breeds cynicism, and to invoke the word "character" is to invite a cynical response. My friends, it is too late in the day for that. Character is destiny, and has been since the Bible, the *Iliad*, and the *Odyssey*. The character of our people, of those who lead us and those who interpret public affairs for us, is the foundation of American democracy.

In this closing year of the century and the millennium, let us try to discipline our common talent for cynicism, to recover a sense of the mystery and wonder of life, and to rededicate ourselves to the renewal of American democracy through the renewal of American character.

May 9, 1994

Advice to Young Americans

Being invited to give a commencement address is an honor and a challenge. It presumes that the speaker has, one way or another, accumulated so much wisdom that it should be shared with a large assembly of persons, and learned persons at that.

But everyone knows that younger Americans are far more knowledgeable, about a great many things, than their elders. At least, that's the way it seemed to me when I was young. And as I have grown less and less young, I begin to realize the limits of my learning—and how much there is in the world and in human experience still to comprehend. Someone once said, "Ignorance is salvageable, but stupid is forever," and I find that validated every day of my life.

There is an important difference between the brute accumulation of facts and the learning that matters most. T. S. Eliot summed it up, many decades ago, with a question that still haunts most American colleges and universities: "Where is the wisdom we have lost in knowledge? Where is the knowledge we have lost in information?" Your education, I am confident, has taught you the difference between the amassing of facts and the learning that matters. The ability to discriminate in that regard is one mark of a truly educated person. You may take that for granted now. But as you move on to careers, to graduate school, to whatever the future holds, you will see it in a different light. You will discover how fortunate you were to attend a school in which education is directed toward the spirit as well as the mind.

It used to be that way in most of our academic institutions, both public and private. But no more. A relentless secularism has purged all but the ceremonial trappings of belief from most universities, even many which still advertise their religious affiliations. And for two generations of college students, the result has been a cheapening, a coarsening, a corruption of education. On many campuses, especially those with the largest endowments and widest influence, the study of literature is no longer a way to commune with noble minds of the past. It is a way to deconstruct all belief, all values, into a rubble of fractured words.

The study of history is no longer a way to learn from the trials and triumphs of those who have gone before us. It is, instead, the means to advance grievances and invalidate tradition.

Political science has become indoctrination. Sociology has become propaganda. Psychology, an invitation to despair.

And theology, which used to be called the queen of the sciences, survives largely as a forum for righteous radicalism of the Left.

None of this should surprise us. When faith in God is driven out of education, much else goes with it. Respect for mankind, for example, both in the aggregate and in the individual. That's all lost.

Respect for the past is lost too. It no longer has anything worth telling us, and so we need not listen. Perhaps you were wondering why this country's education establishment has replaced courses in American history with classes in current events? Wonder no more. Despite the motto of our National Archives, the past is no longer prologue. It is irrelevant at best; at worst, an embarrassment.

Worst of all, when God goes, truth goes. I mean, the very idea of truth, the very possibility of truth, goes out the window. And all else becomes relative. All else. Not just our food preferences in the cafeteria, but our ethics, our moral codes, our ideas of justice and fairness. So guilt and innocence lose their meaning. They, too, become relative. And so do the ethical norms of journalism, in which old-time factual reporting has been largely displaced by interpretation. Which is to say, the replacement of truth by opinion.

The abandonment of the concept of truth has even affected the way we speak, the words we use. Have you noticed that, when celebrities are interviewed, they seldom say "I know" or "I think." Rather, they "feel." "Feeling" has infected our language, top to bottom: Even many in high office "feel" this way or that about policies, laws, and decisions. Some of them even "feel our pain," but that is another matter.

Young people often tell me how they "feel" about various issues. I don't care much how they feel. I do care greatly what they think. I care what they think because I respect them as rational beings. And when they search for truth in a matter, rather than probing their own feelings about things, they show in themselves sparks of the divine intellect.

What, on the other hand, do we reveal about ourselves when we use terms like "alternate lifestyles" in order to avoid the appearance of being judgmental? In a society that has lost the notion of sin, being judgmental is as close as we come to a damnable offense. A couple of years ago, I played host to Charlton Heston, who came to confer with our Members about certain legislation. Whenever Chuck Heston was around, people would make Moses jokes. This was no exception. But it reminded me of something that is no joking matter. It reminded me that, when Moses came down from Mount Sinai with the two stone tablets, they did not contain Ten Recommendations or Ten Suggestions or Ten Pieces of Advice.

They contained commandments. And those commandments were not based on the whims of an irrational deity. Rather, each commandment was based on truths about human nature. Each was grounded in truths about what is beneficial, and what is harmful, for us as human beings. And that is why, when we ignore a commandment, someone eventually gets hurt—because we are running into a fixed truth about what we are and how we are to live.

The most obvious example has been the sexual revolution—the dramatic change, all for the worse, in behavior over the last thirty years or so. This revolution has had no victors, only victims—victims of exploitation, rape, pornography, and most of all, abortion. And all of it was the perfectly predictable consequences of abandoning truth and adopting relativism. Remember, when the

Supreme Court, in 1973, removed all legal protections from children before birth, it did not declare that those children were not
human beings. It did not find that they were not members of the
human species. In other words, it did not assert anything as truth.

Instead, it observed that different people believe different
things about unborn children. And in the face of such disagreement,
our laws had to be neutral. In short, the Court repudiated—not just
what I happen to believe about fetal development—but the very
idea of truth itself.

In the case of abortion, the consequences of that repudiation
have been fatal—literally, fatal—to millions of children. But the
death of truth itself touches every one of us. It touches our pubic
discourse, where words now mean only what we want them to
mean. During the worst of the French Revolution, the Parisian mob
enthroned on the high altar of the Cathedral of Notre Dame a
woman they called "the Goddess of Reason." That was bad enough.
Today, the American cultural revolution enthrones the goddess of
Un-Reason, and she is a cruel mistress.

That has profound implications for the future of our system of
government. As a wise friend of mine, George Weigel, says, for a
good monarchy, all you need is a virtuous king. But for a successful democracy, you need a virtuous people. The Framers of the
Constitution and those who came after them—Adams and his
Federalists, Jefferson and his followers—may have disagreed about
everything from foreign policy to the tax on whiskey. But they all
agreed that virtue was the only possible basis for lasting freedom.
Only a virtuous people, they believed, had the discipline and direction to use freedom rightly and, hence, to preserve it.

That was the lesson those early Americans learned both from
Scripture and from secular history. It helped them make sense of
the rise and fall of empires, from the ancient world to contemporary
upheavals in Europe. And it gave special meaning to their break
with Britain. It should give a special meaning, as well, to your education at this institution dedicated to the pursuit of truth—and to
what you will do with that education after you leave here.

Yes, it's going to matter, to you and your children, whom we elect to public office. Yes, it's going to matter whether their policies are sound or faulty. But the character of the people they govern—your character and that of your children—will matter far more. That character is shaped, in part, in institutions like this—and in homes, schools and, of course, churches throughout America. That shaping, that molding, that leading into right paths is not only a noble spiritual endeavor; it is also a necessary civic enterprise. For upon its success depends the survival of our free institutions.

How should we describe this age in which we live? Addicted to consumption? Jaded? Living for the moment? Scoffing at the eternal verities? Heedless of what Jefferson called "the laws of Nature and of Nature's God"? All that and more. But we aren't the first believers to confront such a society. Peter and Paul did it before us, with less resources and far fewer troops. And they did not have what you and I have: the marvelous mechanisms of democracy, by which a virtuous people can eventually set things straight.

Wonders do happen, and not only in Scripture. Some fifteen years ago, in the late 1970's, when most of today's graduating class were in the second or third grade, America's international situation was every bit as bad as our nation's social situation is now. The voices of sophisticated ignorance declared the American era over. The best we could hope for was coexistence with an expanding Marxist empire and a constricting economy here at home.

It was all a lie. And those who would not accept the lie determined to change the way things were. Here in this country, in Eastern Europe, and in rebel camps in the Third World, men and women refused to submit to history. Instead, they dared to master it. Little more than a decade later, the world was spinning in new directions. The Berlin Wall was in ruins, as was the ideology that had built it.

That revolution in world affairs was not the result of social trends, or climates of opinion, or impersonal forces. It came about because brave and determined individuals made it happen. Each of their decisions, each of their actions, was a stone in the edifice of history.

Now it is time to do the same thing in America's domestic

affairs. Because we believe that, including the power of prayer, individuals make, quite literally, all the difference in the world, we should not underestimate what we have going for us. You should not be discouraged as you set out into this world that is so much out of sync with your views and your values. In these last years of the 1990's, it is more than the Twentieth Century that is coming to an end. The whole order of secular liberalism—built in part by Marx and Engels, in part by Darwin and Freud, by Rousseau and August Compte, by John Dewey and John Maynard Keynes—it is all falling, fading, ebbing, withering away.

We are witnessing the protracted end of mankind's latest attempt, begun two hundred years ago in the French Revolution, to build another Tower of Babel, a heaven on earth. Like all such attempts, it turned hellish. It gave us Nazism, Communism, the cult of the State, the degradation of the individual, the ruin of the family, and now the total breakdown of any rational concept of human sexuality. It gave us, in short, what Paul Johnson, in his magisterial book some years ago, called "Modern Times."

But how quickly do things modern become outdated. This is how false gods fail, not with a bang but a long, slow process of degeneration and deterioration. They are hollow within long before their phony gilding wears away outside. So be not alarmed that, here in America, the forces arrayed against faith and family seem to shine with power and prestige. To paraphrase what John Randolph once said about John C. Calhoun, theirs is the brilliance of a dead mackerel shining in the moonlight.

Anyone with ears to hear can already make out the sound of the future. It rings from the great bells of the Kremlin, so long silenced, that again praise the God of Christendom. It sings in the voices of the underground Christians in places like China and Vietnam. It cries out across America in the demand for the right to pray in the classroom and to honor our Creator in the public square.

Those who have foolishly put their trust in secular liberalism can have the past, with all its ruin to the human body and soul. But we who trust, not in princes or in ourselves, but in the Author and Father of all history, we have . . . the future.

View of the sign and William Allen White quotation above
the "Henry J. Hyde" room in the U.S. Capitol Building.

Afterword

A s the final touches were being put on this book our good friend—the author of the speeches included here and of so much good manifested in countless other ways—died on November 29, 2007. President Bush issued a gracious statement:

> Laura and I are deeply saddened by the death of former Congressman Henry Hyde. From his service in the Navy during World War II until his retirement from the U.S. House of Representatives last year, Henry Hyde led a life devoted to public service. During more than 30 years as a Congressman, he represented the people of Illinois with character and dignity—and always stood for a strong and purposeful America. This fine man believed in the power of freedom, and he was a tireless champion of the weak and forgotten. He used his talents to build a more hopeful America and promote a culture of life. Earlier this month, in recognition of his good and purposeful life, I was proud to award Henry Hyde the Medal of Freedom.
>
> Congressman Hyde's passing represents a great loss to the people of Illinois and our Nation, and our thoughts and prayers are with his family in this sad hour.

I attended the Presidential Medal of Freedom ceremony, held in the White House on November 5th. Bob Hyde was present to accept this high honor on behalf of his father, who was back home in Illinois fighting mightily to recover from heart surgery.

Again, Mr. Bush spoke warm and appropriate words:

> Bob Hyde is here on behalf of his Dad, the Honorable Henry J. Hyde, who was not able to be with us today. Congressman Hyde spent more than three decades as a towering figure on Capitol Hill. But he first made his name in Washington more than

60 years ago. He was on the Georgetown basketball team, and played in the NCAA Eastern championship game in 1943. After college and Navy service in World War II, he returned home to Illinois, and earned a law degree, and made his way into politics. This erudite, scholarly man has walked with kings and kept the common touch. He won 20 elections, and gave steady service to the people of Illinois for 40 years.

In the House, Congressman Hyde rose to the chairmanship of two committees, Judiciary and International Relations. And from the first day, he was a commanding presence, and he was a man of consequence. Colleagues were struck by his extraordinary intellect, his deep convictions, and eloquent voice. In committee and in the House chamber, the background noise would stop when Henry Hyde had the floor.

He used his persuasive powers for noble causes. He stood for a strong and purposeful America—confident in freedom's advance, and firm in freedom's defense. He stood for limited, accountable government, and the equality of every person before the law. He was a gallant champion of the weak and forgotten, and a fearless defender of life in all its seasons.

Henry Hyde spoke of controversial matters with intellectual honesty and without rancor. He proved that a man can have firm convictions and be a favorite of Democrats and Republicans alike.

Henry likes quoting the adage, "Make new friends, but keep the old; one is silver but the other is gold." To so many on Capitol Hill, Henry Hyde's friendship is gold. They're quick to say it's not the same Congress without him—but that we're a better country because he was there. And colleagues will always admire and look up to the gentleman from Illinois, Henry J. Hyde. And, Bob, please tell your Dad a lot of us in Washington love him.

As an admirer, as his friend, I wish Henry Hyde could have held a printed copy of this work—it meant much to him, and not for vainglory. He truly believed in the power of speech, as a man with his talents had every right to believe.

A speech not in this book is one he gave a few years ago at a dinner for the Human Life Foundation, publisher of *The Human Life Review*, the respected scholarly quarterly on abortion and other life

issues. Mr. Hyde received an award named for the *Review*'s
founder, the late James P. McFadden. I found Mr. Hyde's remarks
particularly moving and appropriate that night, and more so now,
reflecting on his own death.

But I think what I will do is read to you something I ran across a
few years ago at the funeral of another great warrior for the
unborn: Joe Stanton up in Boston. And at his funeral there was a
little booklet printed. And it had in it a poem by somebody named
CVS. I don't know who that is. But boy does this apply to Jim
McFadden. So please permit me to share it with you.

Traveling from afar he neared the gate
And seeing no one, paused
Dusty, footsore, spent
Bone tired, if the truth were known,
And rested on his cane.
The gates swung idly there
Inviting any pilgrim inside,
Where all was cool and still.
He felt a peace enfold him
And he knew that he was home
Then, like a great wind they came,
Filling the air with a sound,
A most unlikely regiment of children
As far as the eye could see.
Noisy, babbling, weeping,
A Lilliputian army
Not one, by measure, reached his knee
Calling his name with joy and welcoming
Clutching his coat as if to make him theirs.
Aye, he was theirs,
Had been always.
Fought for them all
With blood and bone and nerve
Those dead, dear children.
All our sons and daughters
The smothered secrets of our public shame

And he would weep
Weep and remember
There is no peace while the red river flows
And mourn those lives, written not in water
But in the martyrs' love that stains the rose.

[A]nd . . . I think of a statement I read on a dedication of a hospital once. And it made—it struck a chord with me—so let me just wind up by leaving this with you: "Those tragedies which break our hearts again and again are not more numerous than the healing influences that mend them. More impressive than the brokenness of our heart is the fact we have a heart, and it's tender enough to suffer. Even the scar tells us of more than the wound we have sustained; it tells us we have prevailed. And all the agony in the world can't erase the fact that a man is born, and life and thought, emotion and choice, love and reason go on inside him."

I want to salute every one of you here for your membership in the greatest organization in the world, the pro-life movement. You know why it's great? No self-interest. Most groups look for shorter workweeks, wider sidewalks, no hammerhead sharks in the district—all sorts of things. But the pro-life movement has no self-interest. It hurls itself on the battlements because it wants to defend the most helpless and vulnerable of God's creatures.

Henry Adams, when he visited the Cathedral at Chartres said, "it embodies the noblest aspirations of mankind; the reaching up to Infinity." That's what the pro-life movement does. That's what you do; and I hope that some day we will all be there and hear the same words that Jim McFadden heard five years ago today when our time comes: "Come beloved of my Father and enter the Kingdom which has been prepared for you since the beginning of time." Thank you so much.

We trust that Henry Hyde has heard those same words, and that he now abides in a place which means more to him than any book could.

Jack Fowler
Publisher, *National Review*
February 2008

Index